D1134533

Wild *about* *the* Garden

Wild about the Garden

Jackie Bennett

FOREWORD BY CAROL KLEIN
INTRODUCTION BY JOHN PERCIVAL

PHOTOGRAPHY BY ANDREA JONES

BOXTREE

In Association with
CHANNEL FOUR TELEVISION CORPORATION

First published in 1998 by Boxtree

an imprint of Macmillan Publishers Ltd
25 Eccleston Place, London SW1W 9NF
and Basingstoke

Associated companies throughout the world

ISBN 07522 2432 8

Text © Jackie Bennett 1998
Photographs © Andrea Jones 1998

The right of Jackie Bennett to be identified as Author of this Work has been asserted by her in accordance with the
Copyright, Designs and Patents Act 1988.

All rights reserved. No part of this publication may be reproduced, stored in or introduced into a retrieval system, or
transmitted, in any form, or by any means (electronic, mechanical, photocopying, recording or otherwise) without the prior
written permission of the publisher. Any person who does any unauthorized act in relation to this publication may be liable to
criminal prosecution and civil claims for damages.

1 2 3 4 5 6 7 8 9 10

A CIP catalogue entry for this book is available from the British Library.

Designed by DW Design
Edited by Charlie Carman
Typeset by SX Composing Ltd, Rayleigh, Essex
Printed and bound in Italy by New Inter Litho

PAGE 3: *Thalictrum delavayi*

Wild About the Garden by Jackie Bennett is a companion to the television series 'Wild About the Garden'

produced for Channel Four by First Circle Films Limited

AUTHOR'S ACKNOWLEDGEMENTS

With special thanks to all at First Circle Films, particularly Maggie Haworth and Clare Batty who cheerfully supplied me
with information for the book despite having their own heavy workload. My thanks also to John Percival, Charlie Carman,
Andrea Jones, Sandy Holton and Mandy Little for their help and encouragement.

PHOTOGRAPHER'S ACKNOWLEDGEMENTS

Special thanks to all those who allowed me and my cameras into their gardens and for their help and hospitality:

Beth Chatto, The Beth Chatto Gardens, Elmstead Market,
Colchester.
Andy and Louise Gill, Moreton-in-Marsh, Gloucestershire.
Andy MacGregor and Katriona Cleghorn, Ben Lawers,
Loch Tay, Scotland.
Mary King, Telegraph Hill, London.
Peter Gregory and all at Westonbirt Arboretum, Gloucestershire.
Steve and Ann McTaggart, Burley, Hampshire.
Daphnie Cushnie, Stockland, Devon.
Bob and Rannveig Wallis, Porthyrhyd, Camarthen, Wales.
Stevie Mort, Fast Rabbit Farm, Nr Dartmouth, Devon.
Toby Abrehart and Val Davies, Wrentham, Suffolk.
Isabelle Van Groeningen, Coleshill, Wiltshire.
Philip Willsher, Compton Acres, Poole, Dorset.
Kim Hurst, The Herbery, Tenbury Wells, Gloucestershire.
Nayla and Ian Green, Dawlish, Devon.
Mike O'Leary, Courtyard Farm, Ringstead, Norfolk.
Henry Head, Norfolk Lavender Farm, Hunstanton, Norfolk.
Tim Smit, John Nelson and all the team at

'The Lost Gardens of Heligan'.
Paul Ingwersen, Ingwersen's Nurseries, Gravetye, East
Grinstead, Surrey.
Terry Wells, Reserve Manager, Gowk Bank, Cumbria.
Tim Leese, Wells-Next-the-Sea, Norfolk.
Nicky and Mark Chaplin, Gunnislake, Devon.
Norman Muddeman, Weston, Suffolk.
Chesil Beach courtesy of the Ilchester Estate, Dorset.
Shelia and Russell Jones, Bournemouth.

Wildlife courtesy of:
Sand Lizard, Chris Davis of the Sand Lizard Breeding Programme.
Hedgehog, Penny and David Rudd, Chester.
Oliver the Tawny Owl, the New Forest Owl Sanctuary, Crow,
Ringwood, Hants.
Crab, Joe Miller at Lulworth Cove, Dorset.
Hover fly and wild flowers, Bill and Sue Acworth, Little Hidden
Hidden Wildflower Farm, Hungerford, Hants.
Otter, the Tamar Otter Sanctuary, Devon.

CONTENTS

Acknowledgements   4
Foreword Carol Klein   6
Introduction John Percival   7

1. WOODLAND   10

Planting a New Woodland ◆ *Making a Woodland-Style Garden* ◆
Coppicing Trees ◆ *Woodland Plants* ◆ *Woodland Wildlife* ◆
Where to See Woodland and Woodland Plants

2. MEADOW   44

Converting a Lawn to Meadow ◆ *Creating a New Perennial
Meadow* ◆ *Meadow Plants* ◆ *Meadow Wildlife* ◆
Where to See Meadows and Meadow Plants

3. WETLAND   70

Making a Pond ◆ *Making a Bog Garden* ◆ *Wetland Plants* ◆
Wetland Wildlife ◆ *Where to See Wetlands and Wetland Plants*

4. SEASHORE   98

Making a 'Seashore' Garden ◆ *Seashore Plants* ◆ *Seashore
Wildlife* ◆ *Where to See Seashore and Seashore Plants*

5. HEDGEROW   124

Planting a Garden Hedge ◆ *Road Verges* ◆
Hedgerow Plants ◆ *Hedgerow Wildlife* ◆
Where to See Hedgerows and Hedgerow Plants

6. MOUNTAIN, MOOR AND HEATH   158

Making a Wild Rock Garden ◆ *Mountain and Moorland Plants* ◆
Heathland Plants ◆ *Mountain and Moorland Wildlife* ◆
Heathland Wildlife ◆ *Where to See Mountain and Moorland Plants*

Useful Addresses and Contacts   188
Further Reading and Reference   188
List of Protected Species   189
Index   191

FOREWORD

HAVE YOU GOT A GARDEN? Do you think it's important? Not just to you and your family and friends, but on a national or even a global scale?

In the British Isles, our gardens comprise 12% of the cultivated land and they cover a larger area than all our nature reserves put together. They are a vastly important national resource in the hands of 15 million caretakers. What every single one of us does with our garden is crucial.

Lots of us who garden have strong memories of the country landscape: meadows full of daisies and poppies, woods thick with bluebells and hedgerows brimming with foxgloves and ferns. We can remember the incessant hum of insects and the soaring song of the lark, but such sights and sounds are becoming rarer by the day. Meadows have been ploughed up for more intense crop production, woods and forest felled to clear the hillsides for sheep to graze. Hedgerows have been ripped out on a massive scale to enable giant machinery to whiz through the bare fields with greater speed and efficiency and every inch of ground to be used to maximize profit.

Yearning for what was is a fruitless and frustrating exercise. We can't turn the clock back. But we can do something positive ourselves, through our own attitude to gardening and what we do in our own backyards.

As we approach the millennium, human society's relationship with nature is one of domination and destruction, whether it's splashing on the weedkiller or melting the polar ice caps. So much gardening is confrontational: pull this out, kill that, cut that back. Why do we do it when the alternatives are so attractive, so easy, so rewarding – so natural?

In our Channel Four series *Wild about the Garden* we meet people who are already gardening in sympathy with nature and others who want to do the same. We visit six different habitats and find out from experts who live and work with them how the widely differing conditions affect the flora and fauna. We also spend time with ordinary gardeners, who through their love of nature have adapted their practices to help their plots thrive. We get to grips with six gardens, each one relating to one of the habitats. We work with the gardeners, and together we explore the ways they can embrace nature and welcome it into their gardens.

Through watching our series and reading Jackie Bennett's clear and definite book, we hope that you too will choose to be Wild about the Garden.

CAROL KLEIN

INTRODUCTION

ALL GARDENERS FIND OUT SOONER OR LATER that you cannot grow a plant in the wrong place. Put a primrose in full sun and it will wither. Plant an alpine in a soggy corner and it will rot. The reason is that all our garden plants are descended, one way or another, from wild ancestors which first evolved by adapting themselves to a particular habitat – damp woodland in the case of the primrose, moist but well-drained mountain screes and crevices in the case of the alpines. They may be selected strains, hybridized and removed a thousand generations from their origins, but if the conditions we provide for them in the garden are very different from those which their distant relatives still enjoy in the wild, they will never flourish.

All our gardens are part of the greater landscape around them. In my own part of the Thames Valley the soil is sandy, with an underlying bed of river gravel. No matter how much compost I dig into it, that soil will never hold water. If I want a perfect lawn I have to resign myself to running a sprinkler all the way through the summer. I have to give the grass top dressings of fertilizer in the spring, mow it once a week during the growing season, spray it with selective herbicides to kill off the weeds, and with pesticides to slaughter the leather-jackets. I may even want to kill off the worms which leave their casts all over the surface, or take extreme measures against the squirrels which dig little holes in the turf.

This is all hard work and very time-consuming. It is also extremely expensive. Worse than that, it is very destructive to the environment – not just to the insects and wildflowers which perish every time I use the sprayer, but because of the hundreds of litres of fuel guzzled up by the mower and the thousands of litres of water which get sprinkled on to the grass, only to turn to vapour in a few minutes of warm sunshine. Multiply those effects by the five million or so lawns in this country and you can see how we gardeners are making quite a significant contribution to worldwide pollution.

Alternatively, I can give up the lawn and grow something else – some plants, say, which are better suited to the conditions prevailing in my garden. I only have to stroll down the road to see what is growing, without any assistance from the petro-chemicals industry, on the well-trodden acres of the nearby common. Despite centuries of degradation, these few acres of scrubby heath still bear some relationship to the wild landscape. There are stands of oak, birch and holly, and tangles of bramble and sloe, interspersed with patches of bracken and mixed grassland. Woodpeckers and sparrowhawks occasionally put in an appearance, and so do many of our native butterflies. If I choose plants related to those which scrape a living here I can make a garden which is in tune with its surroundings.

Admittedly, those wild plants which survive in this suburban savannah are unlikely to win any awards in a horticultural show, but I don't have to restrict myself to them. I can take my pick of plants which flourish in similar dry, slightly acid grasslands in many different countries. And just as the common has areas of woodland, where many shade-loving plants manage to thrive, so even my small garden has different micro-climates – shady places where the soil is moister and more fertile, and I can grow a range of different woodland plants from similar habitats all over the world.

Within a few hundred yards of the common the soil is a deep London clay. It sets rock hard in summer and turns to glutinous sludge in winter, but it holds water far better than the gravel, and in the clay it is possible to grow plants like astilbes which love marshy conditions. With a little effort I could find, within a few minutes' walk, gardens, or fragments of gardens, which have echoes of many other landscapes – a shrubbery like a country hedgerow, a tower block balcony as windswept as a mountain top, with a backyard in its shadow as dark and dank as the deepest forest floor. If I want to know what plants will thrive in those different places, all I have to do is to seek out wild places where the soil, the temperature range, the amount of sunshine, the exposure to wind and rain are much the same.

When I speak of wild places in a British context, I have to qualify what I mean. There is not a single corner of these islands which has not been used or abused by human beings over the last ten thousand years. As soon as the first farmers began to clear the forests and graze their flocks on the hills they also started to change the balance of plants in the landscape, favouring some trees over others in the woodlands, favouring crops over weeds in the arable fields. But for most of that time there were limits to what the farmers could do. Moorland remained moorland and marshes stayed undrained. There were always weeds in the crops; the woods and pastures were full of wildflowers; birds, small mammals and insects which depended on those plants could always find ways of hanging on.

When the Romans brought in the heavy plough, with share and coulter, the pressure on the land increased, and succeeding centuries saw a gradual improvement in agricultural techniques which brought enormous changes to the landscape. In some areas, like the fens or the Somerset levels, great marshes were drained and put down to pasture. In much of the Midlands the network of small hedged enclosures was opened up to medieval ridge and furrow, only to be re-enclosed a few centuries later. But these changes did not happen everywhere. Up to the end of the Second World War there were still huge areas which remained much as they were in Roman times – small fields fenced in with ancient hedgerows, woodlands still growing within their medieval boundaries. There were still wildflowers in the meadows, poppies in the wheat fields, and larks in the sky.

The last fifty years have seen more changes than the previous two thousand. In pursuit of greater productivity, and with the help of modern technology, modern farmers have cleared half the hedgerows in the country. They have wiped out the weeds in the cornfields, ploughed up the meadows and drained the wetlands. They have soaked their crops with so much water that many streams and rivers are threatened with extinction and they have sprayed them with so many pesticides that we begin to fear their effects on human, let alone insect, health. They have given us cheaper food, but they have shifted the natural balance right off the scale, favouring food production to the near exclusion of other forms of life. Meanwhile, thousands of ancient fields and woodlands have disappeared under roads or been swallowed up by new housing estates, still further reducing the pockets of natural habitat where wild plants and animals can survive.

Gardeners have tended to follow the lead of modern farmers, using chemicals and machinery in place of traditional hand labour, to get rid of the weeds, kill the pests and quell the diseases. Like farmers, they have also been able to take advantage of imported plants and modern hybridization techniques and the reward has been a rich harvest of instant colour, flawless lawns, weedless flowerbeds. In the garden, as on the farm, all this progress has been bought at a high price. Many wild flowers, insects, birds and mammals which were commonplace when I was a child have become rarities today.

Fortunately, a few far-sighted individuals have ensured that some of the wild places have survived, as reservoirs for threatened plants and animals. More recently, some farmers have gone over to organic methods, dispensing with chemicals and growing their crops in a way which is far friendlier to nature. Meanwhile in gardens all over the country there are the first signs of a quiet revolution. More and more gardeners are now willing to cut down on the pesticides and reserve patches of their own plots for wildlife. Some have gone further, and established their own wildflower meadows. Others have taken up the fashion for semi-permanent beds of herbaceous perennials. In all these new departures, there are signs of hope for those who care about the environment.

In this book, Jackie Bennett gives us a fascinating account of six different aspects of the British countryside and the wild plants which flourish there – in woods and meadows, hedgerows and marshes, on mountainsides and on the seashore. She shows us how closely our gardens resemble different natural habitats and how we can make make them more sympathetic to natural processes by growing plants from many different parts of the world which enjoy the same conditions. There is a lot of good practical advice on how to achieve this, and plenty of delightful plant portraits to enhance our pleasure in the process. Between us, we gardeners control an astonishing 12 per cent of the cultivated land in this country. If we want to, we can really make a difference, and this book shows us how.

JOHN PERCIVAL

Chapter 1

Wood

land

MANY OF US GREW UP IN A TIME WHEN there seemed to be more deciduous woodlands and certainly more wildflowers. Over the past hundred years, the move away from wood to other forms of fuel such as coal and gas, combined with the switch from hardwoods to plantation softwoods for building, has led to a dramatic decline in the care and management of old woodlands. The canopy of a wood left to its own devices – particularly one that has been managed in the past – will quickly close over. Without selected felling and the filtered sunlight this produces, there can be no carpets of bluebells, stitchwort or snowdrops. The woodland floor will be devoid of sunlight and bereft of flowers.

Yet, while we mourn the loss of these managed woodlands and the habitat they create for plants and wildlife, we often overlook the fact that our own gardens have more

in common with the woodland habitat than we might think. Many of us struggle with shady gardens, where a tall building, a neighbour's fence or a street tree block out the sunlight. Most gardens – even if they have no trees at all – have a shady spot that is often neglected. Instead of viewing these as problem areas, we can look on them positively, as a chance to choose plants that will be happy in this environment. The whole garden – or, at least, part of it – could provide the basis of a woodland garden. The best way to get ideas for creating a woodland garden, or for adapting an existing garden, is first to look at the wild habitat, at how the woodland ecology works, from a full-sized tree down to the flowers and fungi at ground level.

Autumn, Ridley Woods, Hampshire

WILDWOOD

There is a deep and enduring fascination with the idea of wildwood – prehistoric forests that once covered the land before the colonization of man. Since the end of the last Ice Age, approximately eleven thousand years ago, waves of trees have colonized the landscape. Birch probably takes the prize for the first tree to colonize Britain, closely followed by pine. As the climate warmed, hazel, oak, lime, elm, alder, ash, hornbeam and beech made steady progress across the landscape, and by 4500 BC almost the whole of Britain was wooded. It is tempting to think that, since then, human beings have simply been hacking their way through dense trees and undergrowth to grow crops and make settlements, leaving areas

untouched to become true fragments of wildwood. The truth is, settlers from Neolithic times to the present day have been using and removing woodlands for their own needs at a fairly steady rate and virtually no woodlands have escaped human intervention.

The New Forest, Hampshire

By the time of the Domesday Survey of 1086 there was no longer a dense coverage of trees, but there were plenty of woodlands between the settlements, used for everything from keeping pigs to charcoal-burning. In almost every county of Britain there are small, natural woodlands that, even if they do not contain direct descendants of prehistoric trees, have their own particular history, flora and fauna. There are some wonderful old and famous woods, like Burnham Beeches in Buckinghamshire, Epping Forest in Essex and Hayley Wood in Cambridgeshire – and many smaller, local woods. Interestingly, the word *forest* has always meant a place that was subject to special laws (generally the King's) or occasionally a place outside the law. It was more a legal term than a physical one, and often indicated a place for raising and hunting deer rather than denoting trees. Woodland, on the other hand, means land on which trees have grown up naturally, but on which throughout history trees have been felled, replanted and managed by man.

WOODLAND MANAGEMENT

The traditional method of woodland management provided for a huge range of timber products and woodland activities. Coppicing (cutting down the smaller trees to ground level) in five-, ten- or fifteen-year cycles provided wood for fuel, fencing, furniture and charcoal. Larger trees, like oaks, were left to provide timber for houses and shipbuilding. Acorns and beech-nuts provided pannage for livestock, particularly pigs, which were turned into the woods to 'graze' in the autumn and winter. This continual clearing and maintenance allowed woodland plants to thrive in the newly made clearings – particularly those that flower in spring like primroses, which put on leaf growth before the woodland canopy blocks out their sunlight. As the coppiced trees grow taller, the plants become dormant, their energy stored in underground bulbs or in seeds, waiting to burst into life again the next time the wood is coppiced. Without this continual clearing and replanting, a wood cannot support flowers or wildlife.

The classic woodland has a three- or four-tiered structure. At the top is a canopy of tall 'mother' trees, such as oak, elm or wild cherry, and beneath them the smaller trees like hazel and birch. Between these trees there are lower-growing shrubs like elder, holly and hawthorn, which provide dappled shade for the woodland floor layer of primroses, bluebells and violets, along with lichens, mosses and fungi. The ecology of this system works perfectly, allowing light to the woodland floor in winter and spring when the plants are developing and offering shade from the summer sun. In autumn, when the trees shed their leaves, a layer of humus-rich litter builds up that enriches the soil and starts the whole cycle off again. This is the principle of the woodland habitat, and no matter on what scale it is practised the constituent parts are the same.

GARDEN WOODLANDS

One thing on which gardeners will unanimously agree is that no two areas of a garden are the same. Even in the smallest plots, there are variations in the amount of sunshine and shade, the dampness or dryness of the soil and of the soil itself, and it is these variations that give us the clues to what we should be planting. Some of us are lucky enough to have gardens that already contain woodland trees and shrubs, or that back on to natural woods. But many more have gardens that already resemble woodlands, perhaps because of the surrounding buildings or the trees in the street that cast shade over their land. If the garden, or part of it, is naturally shady, it is pointless to struggle against it. It is far better to start thinking of it as a woodland habitat and to put in shade-loving plants. You may need to modify some areas to create a better, woodland-type soil but the chances are that the ingredients are already there – fallen leaves, cool temperatures and lack of direct sunlight.

There are lots of ways in which existing garden features can be adapted to create a woodland habitat. It might simply be a case of taking out one or two existing shrubs where they have been planted too close together, improving the soil beneath them and planting shade-loving plants; or planting a carpet of aconites and snowdrops beneath an existing tree; or utilizing a shady corner by planting ferns and foxgloves. By observing how trees, shrubs, climbers and plants behave in their natural setting it is relatively easy to use both native and exotic species in a way that not only looks more natural but in which they will flourish. Just allowing a clematis or honeysuckle to scramble up a silver birch tree, rather than confining it to a trellis, will give the garden an authentic 'wild' look. Conventional lawns with shrub borders already have all the attributes of a woodland clearing – all we need to do is recognize this and plant accordingly. In fact, in suburban areas on the fringes of large cities, foxes and badgers use gardens in exactly the same way as they would use a natural clearing, for feeding, resting and grooming.

Wood anemones (Anemone nemorosa) *carpet the woodland floor, Westonbirt Arboretum, Gloucestershire*

PLANTING A NEW WOODLAND

You can start a woodland from scratch, planting a bare, open plot with trees and shrubs. If you think of the edge of a wood, where the trees become sparser and eventually give way to grass, the average garden can imitate this 'woodland edge' habitat very successfully.

In a garden setting, there is rarely a full canopy of large trees as we would find in a natural woodland. Instead, smaller trees like birch, rowan or hazel become the top 'tier' and the shrubs become the underplanting. The best woodlands are not dense, dark forests but series of open glades where light reaches the woodland floor and wildlife can flourish. The outer boundaries of the garden are the obvious places to site a new woodland area, where the planting will blend in with the landscape to create a natural transition from the more cultivated areas. If you already have some trees or shrubs in the garden you can use them as a starting point and plant around them.

Colchicum autumnale grows naturally on woodland margins

- ◆ Buy young trees and shrubs when they are between 1 and 2 metres (3–6 ft) high. Look for a strong central upward-growing shoot and a healthy root system. It is best to buy from a specialist tree nursery where you know that the trees will have been cared for in their first year or so or life.

- ◆ Clear the ground of any rubbish or debris. There is no need to dig over the whole area, unless it is full of pernicious weeds like nettles and ground elder – or builder's rubble.

- ◆ Space the trees out 2–3 m (6–10 ft) apart. Dig a hole about 1 m (3 ft) across and deep enough to make sure the tree will sit at the same level as it did in the nursery (shown by the soil mark on the trunk). Loosen the soil in the base of the hole and add a spadeful of garden compost.

- ◆ Put a stake in the centre of the planting hole and hammer it firmly into place. It should reach a point about a quarter to a third of the full height of the tree.

- ◆ Plant the tree next to the stake, adding loose soil around the roots and firming in well. Add more soil to bring it up to ground level. Use a rubber tree-tie with a buffer to hold the tree in place.

- ◆ Water the tree well and check regularly during the first year of growth, loosening the rubber tie as the trunk expands.

CREATING A WOODLAND HABITAT

If you are starting a woodland completely from scratch then be prepared to wait several years to see the results. The new trees will not offer enough shade for woodland plants immediately and it is better to wait until they start to branch out and filter the sunlight before introducing flowers. The most important aspect of any woodland garden is the soil, which should be rich in nutrients, moist but fairly well drained. If there is no natural layer of fallen deciduous leaves, you can dig in leaf mould to open up the soil and create a friable texture. Covering the soil with a layer of chopped bark also helps to retain moisture in the soil and create an instant woodland ecosystem.

Wild garlic (Allium ursinum) *and bluebells enjoy filtered sunlight*

TREES FOR DAMP SOIL

	AVERAGE HEIGHT
Alder (*Alnus glutinosa*)	10 m

Rounded green leaves; yellow or purple catkins, February to April; deciduous

Aspen (*Populus tremula*)   15 m
Pale green leaves which flutter in the wind; small catkins, February/March; deciduous

Elder (*Sambucus nigra*)   6 m
Mid green leaves; creamy-white flowers, June/July; black berries; deciduous

Sallow (*Salix cineria*)   10 m
Downy, grey-green leaves; silvery-white catkins, March/April; deciduous

TREES AND SHRUBS FOR NORMAL TO DRY CONDITIONS

Cherry Plum (*Prunus cerasifera*)   8 m
Shiny green leaves; white blossom, February/March; red or yellow fruit; deciduous

Crab Apple (*Malus sylvestris*)   9 m
Oval leaves; pink or white blossom, May/June; small yellow or red fruit; deciduous

Field Maple (*Acer campestre*)   6 m
Small lobed leaves; inconspicuous flowers; winged fruits; deciduous

Guelder rose (*Viburnum opulus*)   4 m
Green leaves, grey underneath; white blossom, June/July; bright red berries; deciduous

Hawthorn (*Crataegus monogyna*)   9 m
Small, divided leaves; pinkish-white blossom, May/June; bright red berries; deciduous

Hazel (*Corylus avellana*)   6 m
Round, downy leaves; yellow catkins, January to March; autumn nuts; deciduous

Rowan (*Sorbus aucuparia*)   12 m
Green leaves, grey underneath; white blossom, May/June; bright red berries; deciduous

Silver Birch (*Betula pendula*)   12 m
Small oval leaves; yellow catkins, April/May; silvery peeling bark; deciduous

TREES AND SHRUBS THAT TOLERATE ACID SOIL

Alder (*Alnus glutinosa*)	10 m
Aspen (*Populus tremula*)	15 m
Beech (*Fagus sylvatica*)	30 m
Crab Apple (*Malus sylvestris*)	9 m
Hawthorn (*Crataegus monogyna*)	9 m
Juniper (*Juniperus communis*)	4 m
Rowan (*Sorbus aucuparia*)	12 m
Scots Pine (*Pinus sylvatica*)	30 m
Sessile Oak (*Quercus petraea*)	30 m
Silver Birch (*Betula pendula*)	12 m

MAKING A WOODLAND-STYLE GARDEN

Converting a shady part of the garden into a woodland garden is one of the best ways to enhance the garden's own natural tendencies and allows the gardener to grow a really interesting range of plants. Whether the shade comes from existing trees and shrubs or is caused by overhanging buildings, there is a range of native and exotic plants that will enjoy this environment.

GROUNDWORK

◆ The first step in creating a woodland garden is to do the groundwork. This means clearing the ground of bramble, tough grasses, nettles or other perennial weeds before planting. The most ecologically sound way to do this is by sheer hard work, first removing the top growth using a strimmer, scythe or bill-hook and then digging out the roots. There is a range of biodegradable weedkillers you could use to make the job easier, and if you are only going to use them once, it might be an acceptable way of being sure all the weeds are removed. If you prefer not to use any chemicals it may take up to a year to clear all the regrowth. In a small garden it is best to dig out all bramble root, as the tiniest piece will allow the stems to reappear, and it is very invasive.

◆ You might want to retain some of the plants that have occurred naturally in a shady area. Work on the principle that if a particular plant has seeded itself or grown there naturally, it is probably one that is suited to that particular site. Bluebells, wood spurge, cow parsley and ground ivy are examples of the kind of plants that might occur in shady areas – it is always worth identifying them with a plant book before digging them up.

A damp, shady garden creates the ideal habitat for hostas and ferns

◆ If the soil is on the dry side, or just looks exhausted and lacking in nutrients, work in lots of leaf mould – home-made is best, but you can now buy it in bags from garden centres. This will improve the humus content of the soil, make it easier to work and enable it to hold water and nutrients more easily. If you don't have leaf mould, dig in garden compost, spent mushroom compost or any organic material to boost the soil.

◆ If there are any fallen trees or logs in the garden, keep them as part of the woodland area. The wood will soon be covered in fungi and lichen and will be home to insects – all of which will enrich the wildlife profile of your woodland.

CHOOSING PLANTS

Plants for the woodland can either mirror those found in the wild or be drawn from more eclectic sources. The main thing is to go for plants that will fend for themselves, will be happy in the newly created woodland soil and will spread to form effective ground cover and keep weeds at bay.

One of the plants that often struggles in suburban gardens is the lily-of-the-valley (*Convallaria majalis*) with its fragrant drooping white bells. In most flower borders the plants get well and truly roasted and struggle bravely to hold their own, but in a woodland

ABOVE: *Solomon's Seal* (Polygonatum x hybridum)
ABOVE RIGHT: *Camellias grow best in moist, peaty soil*

soil – where they would grow naturally – they get the shade and moisture they crave. Some of the most perfect sightings of lily-of-the-valley are in churchyards, where they may grow against the cool side of a headstone, or nestle against a mossy porch, and it is quite easy to replicate this in the garden, under a north-facing window, for example, or under well-mulched shrubs. As well as the plain green-leafed version there is a variegated form with cream stripes on the leaves called 'Albostriata'. Lily-of-the-valley's large cousin Solomon's seal (*Polygonatum x hybridum*) is another candidate for the woodland garden, and although it is often recommended for dry, shady borders where nothing else will grow, it will be a lot healthier in a soil that can retain some moisture.

Another good group of woodland plants – this time not native to Britain – is the epimediums, clump-forming perennials from south-east Europe and Asia, grown for their beautiful foliage. The one species that has naturalized itself in parts of Britain is the barrenwort (*Epimedium alpinum*), which produces red leaves in spring eventually turning bronze in the autumn. The small, delicate flowers are yellow with red spurs and appear in spring. More widely grown is *E. grandiflorum*, which has larger, long-spurred flowers and is available in rose pink and white cultivars. *E. grandiflorum* 'Nanum' is a pretty dwarf variety with white flowers. There are also several evergreen species including *E.* x *perralchicum*, which has red, bronze and copper markings on the leaves. All the epimediums make good ground covering plants and once established will form substantial clumps. They can also be divided in autumn or spring to make new plants.

BELOW LEFT: *Container-grown ferns are ideal for a damp, shady corner*
BELOW: *Lungwort* (Pulmonaria officinalis)

From North America come the foam flowers (*Tiarella* species), good evergreen perennials with starry spires of pinkish-white flowers in late spring. Tiarellas like a rich, moisture-retentive soil and a cool, shady spot, where the foliage will mottle to an attractive crimson or bronze colour. *T. wherryi* is a native of Tennessee and North Carolina, where it grows in shady ravines and woodlands. It is compact enough for a small garden and the cultivar 'Bronze Beauty' has particularly good, coppery foliage.

Ferns are perhaps the best known and most useful woodland garden plants. There are ferns to suit just about every situation, but those that like the classic cool, shady, moist conditions of a woodland include the evergreen hart's tongue fern, the deciduous lady fern and the Japanese painted fern.

The hart's tongue (*Asplenium scolopendrium*) has wide, shiny strap-like fronds that unfurl to make a clump about 60 cm (2 ft) across, which stay looking good through most of the winter. The lady fern (*Athyrium filix-femina*) is easy to grow and has long

filigree fronds, which despite its diminutive appearance at first can soon reach 1 m (3 ft) across. There are literally hundreds of named forms, including several dwarf and miniature varieties. The Japanese painted fern (*A. niponicum* var. *pictum*) is a more decorative plant with triangular fronds that display a range of colour according to the season. The young fronds have deep wine-red ribs and soft grey leaflets and as they mature turn from blue to dark green. Ferns can adapt to most soil pH levels, but the lady fern and the Japanese painted fern have a preference for acid soil.

Japanese maple (Acer palmatum var. heptalobum)

A fairly unusual ground-cover plant is *Omphalodes cappadocica*, a native of the shady chestnut and hazel woods of Turkey and Georgia, but which is quite at home in moist, shady gardens. It forms a creeping mass of heart-shaped leaves and sprays of delicate forget-me-not type flowers in late spring. It is evergreen, but the foliage can be killed off by a hard frost. The cultivar 'Cherry Ingram' is particularly hardy and has deeper mauve flowers than the species. 'Starry Eyes' is a pretty cultivar with white edges to the blue flowers.

Also at home in moist, shady sites are the pulmonarias or lungworts, which are one of the best ground-covering perennials. *Pulmonaria longifolia* forms dense clumps of long, narrow spotted leaves and bears bright blue flowers in spring. The leaf blotching is even more marked on *P. saccharata* and sometimes covers the whole leaf. The Argentea group have narrow silvery white leaves with green edges and are available in a range of colours from white to deepest pink.

For winter interest, the woodland garden should include hellebores, whether one of the native species or one of the many garden cultivars. In British woodlands one of the most prominent winter plants is the stinking hellebore (*Helleborus foetidus*), which not only makes its mark with its bold foliage and purple-rimmed flowers, but also with its strong and quite disagreeable smell. Its smaller cousin, the green hellebore (*H. viridis*), does not have the purple rims to the flowers and is usually found in the damper pockets of the woodland. Of the garden hellebores, the Lenten rose (*H. orientalis*) is the most popular, with large saucer-shaped flowers that shade from palest green to deep rose-pink or purple. All like the same deep, moist soil and at least partial shade. Once planted, hellebores do not like to be disturbed for many years.

MAINTAINING THE WOODLAND GARDEN

◆ After planting, water new plants in thoroughly. Once established they should not need further watering, but in the first summer it is wise to check that new plants have not dried out.

◆ All the woodland plants will benefit from a mulch of chopped bark or leaf mould after planting. This helps to keep their roots cool and conserve moisture. Mulching is doubly important if the area will not get a natural covering of autumn leaves. An annual mulch will encourage beneficial insects and get the whole woodland ecosystem up and running.

◆ The perennial plants listed here will spread to form substantial clumps or patches in a year or two. It is better to over-plant, even if it means pulling up some of the more vigorous species in subsequent years. Some will self-seed and it is worth looking out for seedlings that can be moved to any bare patches. Hardy perennials can be lifted and divided in autumn or early spring.

GROUND-COVERING PLANTS FOR THE WOODLAND GARDEN

	HEIGHT X SPREAD
Lily-of-the-Valley (*Convallaria majalis*)	15 cm (6 in) x 30 cm (12 in)
Broad, mid-green leaves, highly scented waxy white bell flowers, April/May; perennial rhizome. Note: All parts of the plant are poisonous.	
Convallaria majalis 'Albostriata'	15 cm (6 in) x 30 cm (12 in)
Striped green and white leaves; scented, waxy white flowers, April/May; perennial rhizome. Note: All parts of the plant are poisonous.	
Solomon's Seal (*Polygonatum* x *hybridum*)	1.2 m (4 ft) x 60 cm (2 ft)
Arching stems; glossy leaves; white dropping flowers, May; perennial rhizome. Note: all parts of the plant are poisonous.	
Barrenwort (*Epimedium alpinum*)	25 cm (10 in) x 30 cm (12 in)
Young leaves are bronze, older leaves red; dainty yellow flowers with red spurs, March to May; herbaceous, carpeting perennial	
Epimedium grandiflorum	25 cm (10 in) x 30 cm (12 in)
Young growth is bright green, turning bronze; rose-pink flowers with long spurs, April/May; herbaceous perennial	
Epimedium grandiflorum 'Nanum'	20 cm (8 in) x 30 cm (12 in)
Red and green foliage; white flowers, April/May; herbaceous perennial	

Epimedium perralchicum   40 cm (16 in) x 30 cm (12 in)
Young leaves are red turning green; yellow flowers with short spurs, April/May;
evergreen perennial

Foam Flower (*Tiarella wherryi*)   15 cm (6 in) x 30 cm (12 in)
Green leaves with dark red mottling; pinkish-white flower spires, May/June;
evergreen perennial

Tiarella wherryi 'Bronze Beauty'   15 cm (6 in) x 30 cm (12 in)
Bronze/copper foliage; pink or white flower spires, May/June; evergreen perennial

Hart's Tongue Fern (*Asplenium scolopendrium*)   40 cm (16 in) x 60 cm (24 in)
Bright green, strap-shaped fronds; evergreen

Lady fern (*Athyrium filix-femina*)   50 cm (20 in) x 30 cm (12 in)
Pale green, lacy fronds; deciduous

Japanese Painted Fern (*Athyrium niponicum* var. *pictum*) 30 cm (12 in) x 30 cm (12 in)
Silvery-grey fronds with purple ribs; deciduous

Omphalodes cappadocica   25 cm (10 in) x 40 cm (16 in)
Glossy heart-shaped leaves; sprays of tiny bright blue flowers,
March to May; perennial rhizome

Omphalodes cappadocica 'Cherry Ingram'   25 cm (10 in) x 40 cm (16 in)
Heart-shaped leaves; sprays of small mauve flowers, April/May; perennial rhizome

Omphalodes cappadocica 'Starry Eyes'   25 cm (10 in) x 40 cm (16 in)
Heart-shaped leaves; sprays of blue flowers with white margins,
April/May; perennial rhizome

Pulmonaria longifolia   30 cm (12 in) x 45 cm (18 in)
Long, narrow leaves with white spots; bright blue flowers, March to May;
herbaceous clump-forming perennial

Pulmonaria saccharata   30 cm (12 in) x 60 cm (24 in)
Blotched white and green leaves; flowers are pink in bud, opening to a purplish pink,
March to May; herbaceous clump-forming perennial

Stinking Hellebore (*Helleborus foetidus*)   75 cm (30 in) x 60 cm (2 ft)
Green cup-shaped flowers with purple rims, February/March; evergreen perennial.
Note: Unpleasant smell, all parts of the plant are poisonous

Green Hellebore (*Helleborus viridis*)   30 cm (12 in) x 30 cm (12 in)
Dark green palmate leaves; green saucer-shaped flowers, January; deciduous
perennial. Note: All parts of the plant are poisonous

Lenten Rose (*Helleborus orientalis*)   45 cm (18 in) x 45 cm (18 in)
Deeply divided leaves; flushed pink saucer-shaped flowers, February/March;
semi-evergreen perennial. Note: All parts of the plant are poisonous.

COPPICING TREES

Coppicing is one of the oldest forms of woodland management, and the one that is most applicable to the smaller garden. In a traditional woodland, there would be a quantity of large 'standard' trees, left to grow to full height for timber, interspersed with coppiced trees, which were cut down to ground level after a certain number of years. The tree stump left by coppicing throws up long straight shoots, known as 'spring' or 'underwood', which grow remarkably quickly and can produce usable poles after even one year.

Coppiced alder produces several straight stems from the base

Most trees, including willows, oaks, hornbeam, hazel, maple, wych-elm, ash, elder and alder, are suitable for coppicing – cherries, pine and poplar are the exceptions because they do not readily produce new growth. Different woods were coppiced for different uses, with a different cycle of management. The Romans recommended cutting chestnut at five-yearly intervals (sweet chestnut was introduced to Britain in the Roman period) and oak at seven years. Willow and hazel, which grow more quickly, can be cut after one or two years to produce flexible lengths for hurdles and baskets. Willow and hazel rods were also used for wattling in timber-framed houses. Coppiced woodlands contained a variety of species, so that there would always be some underwood to be cut and sold every year – an important part of the local economy.

Coppicing does peculiar things to a woodland: it produces years when lots of light reaches the woodland floor, followed by years of shade as the wood grows upwards and is covered in foliage. These are ideal conditions for the flushes of spring flowers we associate with woodlands: carpets of primroses, oxlips, wood anemones and bluebells. If the light were more continuous, other non-woodland species like grasses and meadow plants would invade. Where a woodland has been managed for timber only and there is only one dominant species, such as oak or beech – however magnificent in themselves – the woodland flora will be poorer.

GARDEN COPPICING

Cutting garden trees down to ground level and allowing new shoots to spring up from the base is one way of keeping them to a manageable size and it is a particularly good way of dealing with trees that are not a particularly good shape. Coppicing one or two trees will instantly change the environment of that particular area of the garden, creating more open areas, perhaps allowing paths to be made between the trees and opening up areas that were previously dark and uninviting. The coppiced trees will not, of course, produce blossom or berries, so you need to be selective, retaining some taller trees to give a good display.

◆ Choose small trees and those that are already multi-stemmed. This makes the cutting process easier – cutting down large trees should be done only by those with considerable experience.

◆ Do the cutting in winter when the tree is dormant.

◆ Use a strong pruning saw (or good pruners for small stems) to cut the stems off 8–10 cm (3–4 in) above ground level. Take off all the stems to leave a stump or 'stool'.

◆ Repeat the coppicing every three to seven years. How often you cut is a matter of personal preference and it is fun to experiment with different types of tree, noting how many years each species takes to produce any usable wood. The cut poles may be used as tree stakes or chopped up for firewood. Thicker wood makes good fencing posts.

Woodland trees were pollarded to keep new growth away from browsing livestock

POLLARDING

At the woodland edges and along roadsides where trees would have been vulnerable to grazing livestock, coppicing was not feasible. A different cutting regime developed which produced the same straight poles but at a different height. The trunk of the tree was cut at between 2 and 5 m (6–15 ft) to keep the new growth well out of reach of cattle and deer. Pollarding was usually carried out on young trees and repeated every ten, fifteen or twenty years. It is not a technique suited to small gardens, but where there is a line of beech, elm, oak, willow or lime, for example either side of a driveway, it is a visually unusual way of keeping the trees to a manageable size. Pollarding is a skilled technique, best carried out by qualified arboriculturists or experienced foresters.

PATHWAYS AND GLADES
IN THE COPPICED WOOD

Cutting down trees to ground level often changes the vistas within a garden and might invite the gardener to make a path through the trees or to set a seat in a newly created woodland glade. A woodland path needs to be in keeping with the natural surroundings and hard landscaping, such as bricks or paving, will probably look out of place. The most sympathetic materials are of woodland origin, such as chopped bark, which is available from garden centres and some recycling organizations. Stepping-stones made of slices of tree trunk can be set at regular intervals, although they will become slippery in wet weather. Where coppicing has produced a naturally occurring glade, leave the area uncultivated for a while to see what plants start to appear. Depending on the soil and the amount of light, meadow plants and grasses might colonize and the grass could be left long as a mini-meadow (see pp. 52-3). If the area already has the shade of larger trees then the falling leaves will create a more conventional woodland environment and woodland plants can be introduced. If there is room, put a seat into one corner of the glade to make the most of the dappled sunlight and as a place to sit and watch the wildlife.

Hydrangeas make an informal edging to a timber path

WOODLAND PLANTS

"To do it rightly, we must group and mass as Nature does.
Though we may enjoy a single flower (. . .) here and there,
the true way is to make pretty colonies of plants."

WILLIAM ROBINSON,
THE WILD GARDEN, 1870

In a woodland setting, the individual plants are less important than the effect that can be achieved by planting groups of the same species. In nature, this is nearly always the case. An individual bluebell is a limp, unprepossessing flower but when we see the plant massed together in a woodland setting the full impact of its colour and form becomes apparent. It seems a nonsense that plant breeders should have tried to produce bigger and brighter bluebells that stand up like sentinels to

Bluebell wood, Wareham, Dorset

make them hold their own in the flower bed. In the wild, a flower is rarely seen in isolation, and by understanding the way that plants arrange themselves in nature we can start to make our plants look and feel at home in the garden.

THE SPRING MESSENGERS

Woodland plants appear predominantly – though not exclusively – in the spring, before the overhead canopy has shaded out their source of sunlight. So, in any woodland areas of the garden, it makes sense to direct our efforts towards getting a good spring display, perhaps with a later flush of autumn flowers, and bulbs for winter. The deciduous woodland in spring is cool and damp underfoot, but surprisingly light and provides exactly the right conditions for several groups of flowers. Of these the best known is the primrose (*Primula vulgaris*), which grows in the humus-rich soil of old woodlands and wherever there is a pocket of shade to provide pro-tection from the scorching summer sun and enough moisture to stop the roots from drying out. In other words, you don't need a full-blown wood to grow primroses, but neither will they be happy in a south-facing border. There are many nooks and crannies in the garden where primroses will flourish: on the north-facing bank of a ditch or mound, between leafy

Wild primroses (Primula vulgaris)

summer perennials, which will grow up above them and protect them from the sun, in the damp soil on the eastern or northern edge of a pond, or under small deciduous trees, such as hazel, cherry or plum. In the wild, primroses often grow along streams, mingling happily with celandines and dog violets.

 P. vulgaris is not the only member of the primula family to enjoy cool, moist conditions. Many of the garden cultivars, particularly the older, cottage garden favourites like the lilac 'Lilacina Plena' and the double white 'Alba Plena' will do well and, of course, the wild oxlip (*P. elatior*) is a natural inhabitant of damp woodlands (now confined to a few old coppiced woods in East Anglia). Don't confuse this plant with the cowslip, which prefers drier more open conditions (see p.63). Primroses need to be planted *en masse* to have any effect and they always look better when there is little soil to be seen between each plant. If the conditions are right, they will spread slowly by seed dispersal, but plants may also be lifted and divided after flowering as long as they are replanted straight away.

If you need to improve the primrose's environment, the simplest way is to mulch around the plants in autumn with a well-rotted manure, garden compost or chopped bark. This will help to retain the moisture in the soil and provide a cool habitat for them to grow, although it cannot compensate for them having been planted in too hot or dry a position to begin with.

Just after the primroses comes the white wood anemone (*Anemone nemorosa*), usually an April flower of copses, clearings and scrubby woodland. Again, they are happiest in a heavy, moisture-retentive soil but can found growing in both acid and alkaline conditions. There are many pretty garden forms of the wild plant in shades of pink and blue. One of the oldest cultivars is 'Robinsoniana', which has large pale lavender-blue flowers and is named after William Robinson, who is said to have found it growing at the foot of a wall in the Oxford Botanic Gardens. Larger and deeper coloured still is 'Alleni', which looks pretty even when the flowers are closed because of the rosy-pink undersides to the petals. There is also a yellow wood anemone (*A. ranunculoides*), which has a scattered distribution in the wild, but is popular with gardeners. It has really bright buttercup yellow flowers and spreads easily, even rampantly, so care needs to be taken in small gardens.

The bluebell (*Hyacinthoides non-scripta*) is the species that has adapted itself most successfully to coppiced woodlands, but as the woods have declined, so has the bluebell. In many urban areas, the only hint that once there were bluebell woods for spring walks and gatherings is a street named Endymion Terrace (the original Latin name was *Endymion non-scripta*) or Bluebell Close. Yet all is not lost. Bluebells are – as any gardener who has introduced them will tell you – an opportunist species. They will spread into new plantations and survive on banks and slopes that were once tree-covered. They don't seem to need shade, although they will clump up more aggressively under the cover of shrubs or trees. They dislike really dry conditions but will grow happily at a woodland edge in the company of stitchwort, yellow archangel and wild garlic. Wild or ramsons garlic (*Allium ursinum*) can be spoken of in the same breath as the bluebell. Both are rampant woodland bulbs, the one catching the eye with its vibrant colour, the other the nose with its smell. The unmistakable aroma of garlic given off by the leaves is not everyone's idea of a companionable garden plant but the starry white flowers are pleasant enough. Still, in the average-sized garden, both plants might give way to other less dominant species.

One group of non-native plants that deserves consideration for the spring woodland garden is the erythroniums or dog's-tooth violets. Not at all related to our native violets and mostly hailing from the cooler states of North America, they are pretty flowers with mottled foliage that are perfectly suited to a damp, shady hollow or any patch of humus-rich soil. The bright yellow *Erythronium americanum* (or trout lily, as the Americans know it) is a common woodland wildflower of New England and looks quite at home in British gardens. Likewise, *E. dens-canis* (the dog's-tooth violet) has white or purple swept-back petals and makes an attractive carpet of flowers beneath deciduous shrubs like viburnums and daphne.

SUMMER ON THE WOODLAND EDGE

Take a walk down any lane bordering woodland in early summer and you will catch a glimpse of a host of flowers flourishing in the light shade and dappled sun of the woodland edge. This is the transition zone between the full shade and moisture of the wood interior and the open grassland of field or meadow.

It is a habitat intrinsic to many gardens where trees or shrubs give way to an open lawn or wide border and where these typical semi-woodland plants will feel at home. The soil tends to be drier at the woodland edge, but the trees still offer some protection from the heat of the summer sun. It is where we find pink and white campion, bugle, yellow archangel, deadnettles, foxgloves, nettle-leafed bell-flowers and columbine – all of which can be grown successfully in gardens alongside their cultivated relatives.

Red campion (*Silene dioica*) – which is actually pink – gives its best display from late spring to early summer but will go on flowering intermittently until the autumn. It is not fussy about soil as long as it gets shade for some part of the day. It is a good nectar supplier for butterflies. It is often found growing in the vicinity of white campion (*S. latifolia* subsp. *alba*) and the two will hybridize to produce pale pink flowers, although the night-scented white campion prefers a drier more open position. Both are perennial plants and will increase easily by natural spreading or seed dispersal. The red campion has a long history in gardens, where it can form part of a shady border of perennials or be grown more like a meadow plant among long grass. There is also a fuller-petalled, double version called 'Flore Pleno' which forms a good border clump, and has pretty, deep-rose-coloured flowers.

Foxgloves (*Digitalis purpurea*) are typical woodland edge plants, with a preference for acid soil. In the wild, foxgloves can be found growing in an amazingly diverse range of environments from the sandy margins of southern conifer plantations to exposed, rocky scree slopes in the north. As plants they look as if they flourish on neglect and in a way this is how they work best in the garden – as marginal plants, set in the poor soil beneath a wall, just outside a picket fence or at the edge of a shrub border among ferns (the male fern *Dryopteris filix-mas* prefers a light, sandy soil and does not need the typical damp fern habitat) . The purple-spotted flowers of the foxglove are a magnet to bees, which disappear into the deep tubes to reappear moments later covered in pollen. White foxgloves are not uncommon in the wild and a small yellow species (*Digitalis lutea*) has become naturalized in Britain. Garden forms are infinitely varied and the popular colours seem to be soft pinks and apricots. Foxgloves are biennial and can be sown from seed in late summer to flower the following year. Once introduced, though, they rarely need replanting and will self-seed around the garden very successfully.

From late spring to midsummer, a conspicuous yellow nettle-leafed plant may be found in woodland copses and in gardens. The yellow archangel (*Lamium galeobdolon*), from the same genus as the pink and purple deadnettles, is a perennial plant, which is very

Foxgloves (Digitalis purpurea)

attractive to bees and which in the right conditions will form quite substantial – even invasive – clumps. It is becoming rare in the wild, found in only a few eastern county

Cerinthe major

locations, but happily has found favour with gardeners, particularly the variegated-leafed 'Florentinum'. There are also one or two forms that will not spread so rampantly, such as 'Silver Carpet' and 'Hermann's Pride'.

Several of the cranesbill family are useful summer additions to the woodland-edge habitat. The bloody cranesbill (*Geranium sanguineum*) likes light, well-drained soil and has bright purplish-pink flowers. If the ground is slightly damper, dusky cranesbill (*G. phaeum*) will do well. Its almost sombre, dark purple flowers earned it the local name of 'mourning widow'. The wood cranesbill (*G. sylvaticum*) has pinky, veined flowers and, as its name suggests, is happiest in the classic woodland habitat of humus-rich soil and dappled shade. Most of the cranesbills or hardy geraniums – including their garden cousins – are hardy, easy-care perennials which, once planted in the right place, will flourish for years. *G. macrorrhizum* is a species from southern Europe that has been adopted by British gardeners since the seventeenth century, mainly because of its ability to grow in places where little else will. This is the cranesbill to choose if you have dry soil beneath a hungry oak tree or on a shady bank. It makes good ground cover, with magenta flowers throughout the summer. The leaves are very aromatic and it was used to extract oil of geranium for the perfume industry. One of the few annual hardy cranesbills is herb-robert (*G. robertianum*) a common plant of woodland margins, which is excellent for covering dry, stony soil. All the cranesbills have characteristic long arching stalks that hold the beak-shaped seed pods, from which they take their name.

A favourite cottage garden plant, but one that is often misunderstood in the garden, is the columbine (*Aquilegia vulgaris*). We know it best as a summer border plant, yet it is more naturally at home in a woodland clearing or on a shady, grassy verge. In open sun, the dainty, maidenhair-fern foliage will become singed and brown and it may grow to only a fraction of its full height. Aquilegias don't need the deep, fertile woodland soil and are happiest on the thinner soils of the woodland edge.

Columbines take their name from the Latin for dove, *columba*, and the swept-back petal spurs are thought to resemble the wings of a dove. It has lots of affectionate local names such as Granny's bonnet and doves-at-a-fountain, and the wild purple forms have crossed with garden plants to produce an almost infinite variety of colours. Packet seed is notoriously unreliable and only a few named varieties, such as the frothy, ice-cream coloured 'Nora Barlow', are guaranteed to come up as intended. If you can get plants of the original species they are worth planting but don't be surprised if, in the following years, the seedlings produce plants in shades of cream, apricot yellow and crimson. This is typical of the promiscuous aquilegia and actually one of its charms.

AUTUMN BULBS AND BERRIES

Colour in the autumn woodland comes from the turning of the leaves and from the bounty of fruit borne by the species in the shrub layer. By including mountain ash or rowan trees (*Sorbus aucuparia*), guelder rose (*Viburnum opulus*), crab apples and wild cherries the garden can be full of bright berries from August to November. The real essence of an autumn woodland, however, lies at the foot of the trees, in the deep layer of fallen leaves and fungi. We do not expect to see many woodland flowers at this time of year but some plants are ideally suited to the cooler temperatures and shafts of weaker sunlight that signal the changing of the season. Among these is the autumn cyclamen (*Cyclamen hederifolium*), also called the ivy-leafed sow-bread, which has naturalized in Britain and is widely grown in gardens. It is a woodland plant and its silvery-marked foliage looks at its finest among fallen beech or oak leaves, although it will also grow in more open, rocky habitats. *C. purpurascens* is also grown in gardens and thrives in a moist alkaline soil. Its deep purple flowers are scented and the leaves are rounded to heart-shaped, easily distinguishable from *C. hederifolium*. The autumn-flowering meadow saffron (*Colchicum autumnale*) is not strictly a woodland plant, but in the garden it will thrive in the grass of a woodland clearing. In the wild it grows in grassy meadows and on woodland margins.

Autumn cyclamen
(Cyclamen hederifolium)

WINTER WOODLANDERS

When we think of winter flowers we think of snowdrops, breaking through a layer of snow or just pushing their heads above a covering of partially decayed leaves and ground ivy. Perhaps it is the purity of their colour set against the inevitable late winter shabbiness of the woodland floor that enchants us. Whatever it is, they have become the epitome of new beginnings (although they rarely appear at New Year) and seem to be have been a part of the garden and the natural landscape for ever. This, though, is not quite the case. *Galanthus nivalis* was certainly introduced some time in the Middle Ages, some say by monks travelling in the plant's native upland, even alpine, parts of southern Europe. Certainly they seem to be common in and around monasteries and have a close association with churchyards. In many areas they are known as Candlemas bells, flowering as they do in time for the Christian Feast of the Purification of the Virgin Mary on 2 February. They were first noticed growing 'wild' in the 1770s in the western counties of Gloucestershire and Worcestershire, and they seem to naturalize most easily in the milder, wetter parts of Britain. Their natural habitat is in damp woodlands, copses and beside streams and they are happiest in association with deciduous trees, particularly where there has been coppicing. As a garden plant, the commonest mistake is to set them into an ordinary border, where they are starved of moisture and of humus. They love to push their way up through a leaf litter of oak, beech or hazel leaves and given this moist, shady environment will develop into a natural carpet. There are probably a hundred different snowdrop species, hybrids and cultivars for gardens, but care is needed as some of the species have totally different requirements from *G. nivalis*. As a general rule, *G. nivalis* cultivars, such as the double 'Flore Pleno' and the boldly marked 'Viridapicis', will enjoy the same woodland conditions as the original species, but other species, such as *G. elwesii*, grow best in dry, limy soil on an open site.

Snowdrops (Galanthus nivalis) – the essence of winter

Like the spring flowers, the winter woodlanders look most at home when grown in quantity and with other compatible species. Snowdrops combine effortlessly with winter aconites (*Eranthis hyemalis*), which can look contrived if planted on their own. Aconites are another 'wild' introduction – arriving from Europe before the sixteenth century and now naturalized in almost every county of England and Wales. The seed can be difficult to sow successfully so it is best to buy tubers for planting. Once established, both snowdrops and aconites will seed and spread naturally, aided by early-flying insects attracted to their unseasonable scent. They can also be grown in the company of sweet violet (*Viola odorata*). This little purple flower comes into its own as the snowdrops and aconites are finishing, although it may have flushes of flowers any time between November and May, depending on local climate. It is a flower of old woodlands, enjoying the dappled shade and woodland floor environment. The deep colour and seductive scent of the violet has ensured its association with love and affairs of the heart. It was Napoleon who was reputed to have said, after his banishment to Elba, that he would return in the spring, with bunches of violets for his beloved Josephine. The less romantically named early dog violet (*V. reichenbachiana*) also thrives in a damp, shady setting.

SPRING PLANTS FOR DAMP, WOODLAND SOILS

	HEIGHT X SPREAD
Primrose (*Primula vulgaris*)	15 cm (6 in) x 23 cm (9 in)

Deeply veined leaves; pale yellow, lightly scented flowers, March/April; perennial

Oxlip (*Primula elatior*)	20 cm (8 in) x 15 cm (6 in)

Veined, hairy leaves; small pale yellow flowers, April/May; perennial

Trout Lily (*Erythronium americanum*)	20 cm (8 in) x 20 cm (8 in)

Mottled green and brown leaves; single bright yellow flowers, April; perennial

Dog's-tooth Violet (*Erythronium dens-canis*)	20 cm (8 in) x 15 cm (6 in)

Mottled green and brown leaves; single purple flowers with swept-back petals; perennial tuber

Wood Lily (*Trillium ovatum*)	25 cm (10 in) x 45 cm (18 in)

Diamond-shaped green leaves; small, three-petalled flowers changing from white to pink, April/May; perennial rhizome

Trillium erectum	40 cm (16 in) x 30 cm (12 in)

Diamond-shaped green leaves; small, three-petalled crimson flowers, April/May; perennial rhizome

SPRING PLANTS FOR AVERAGE WOODLAND SOILS

Bluebells (*Hyacinthoides non-scripta*)	40 cm (16 in) x 30 cm (12 in)

Linear leaves; violet blue nodding bell-shaped flowers, April/May; perennial bulb

Ramsons Garlic (*Allium ursinum*)	20 cm (8 in) x 30 cm (12 in)

Broad leaves with strong garlic aroma; large, rounded umbel of white starry flowers, April to June; perennial bulb

Wood Anemone (*Anemone nemorosa*)	15 cm (6 in) x 30 cm (12 in)

Deeply divided leaves; white cup-shaped flowers, March to May; perennial rhizome

Anemone nemorosa 'Robinsoniana'	15 cm (6 in) x 30 cm (12 in)

Large pale lavender flowers, March to May; perennial rhizome

Anemone nemorosa 'Allenii'	15 cm (6 in) x 30 cm (12 in)

Large lavender flowers, paler on the outside, March to May; perennial rhizome

Yellow Wood Anemone (*Anemone ranunculoides*)	15 cm (6 in) x 30 cm (12 in)

Divided leaves; small, yellow, buttercup-type flowers, March to May; perennial rhizome

SUMMER PLANTS FOR THE WOODLAND EDGE

Red Campion (*Silene dioica*)	60 cm (24 in) x 23 cm (9 in)

Linear to oval leaves; bright rose-pink flowers, May to September; perennial

Foxglove (*Digitalis purpurea*)	1–1.5 m (3–5 ft) x 60 cm (2 ft)

Large, soft grey-green leaves; spires of purple tubular flowers, spotted interiors, May/June; biennial. Note: All parts of the plant are poisonous.

Yellow Foxglove (*Digitalis lutea*) 1 m (3 ft) x 60 cm (2 ft)
  Glossy, dark green leaves; spires of pale yellow flowers; May/June; perennial

Bloody Cranesbill (*Geranium sanguineum*) 25 cm (10 in) x 23 cm (9 in)
  Deeply cut leaves; bright reddish-purple flowers, July/August; perennial

Dusky Cranesbill (*Geranium phaeum*) 60 cm (24 in) x 45 cm(18 in)
  Broad dark green leaves; dark purple flowers, May to September; evergreen

Herb-Robert (*Geranium robertianum*) 20 cm (8 in) x 15 cm(12 in)
  Fern-like leaves; small bright pink flowers, May to September; annual

Yellow Archangel (*Lamium galeobdolon*) 60 cm (2 ft) x 1 m (3 ft)
  Heart-shaped leaves; tubular yellow flowers, July; evergreen perennial

Columbine (*Aquilegia vulgaris*) 45 cm (18 in) x 30 cm (12 in)
  Bluish-green lacy foliage; violet-blue or purple nodding flowers with hooked spurs, June; perennial

  Aquilegia vulgaris 'Nora Barlow' 45 cm (18 in) x 30 cm (12 in)
  Green lacy foliage; three-tone pink, lime green and white double flowers, June; perennial

AUTUMN AND WINTER FLOWERS FOR THE WOODLAND FLOOR

Snowdrop (*Galanthus nivalis*) 15-20 cm (6–8 in) x 15 cm (6 in)
  Grey-green linear leaves; white slightly scented nodding flowers with green marking, February; perennial bulb

  Galanthus nivalis 'Flore Pleno' 20 cm (8 in) x 15 cm (6 in)
  Large double white flowers, February; perennial bulb

Winter Aconite (*Eranthis hyemalis*) 10 cm (4 in) x 15 cm (6 in)
  Green leaf rosettes; bright yellow cup-shaped flowers, February; perennial

Sweet Violet (*Viola odorata*) 7.5 cm (3 in) x 15 cm (6 in)
  Heart-shaped leaves; scented violet flowers, February to April and sometimes intermittently in autumn; perennial

Early Dog Violet (*Viola reichenbachiana*) 7.5 cm (3 in) x 15 cm (6 in)
  Heart-shaped leaves; scented flowers, March to May; perennial

Autumn Cyclamen (*Cyclamen hederifolium*) 15 cm (6 in) x 23 cm (9 in)
  Heart-shaped grey-green leaves marked with silver; deep pink flowers, August to November; perennial tuber. Note: Tuber is poisonous.

Cyclamen purpurascens 10 cm (4 in) x 10 cm (4 in)
  Rounded green leaves; rose pink fragrant flowers, July to September; perennial tuber. Note: Tuber is poisonous.

Meadow Saffron (*Colchicum autumnale*) 15 cm (6 in) x 10 cm (4 in)
  Small lilac goblet-shaped flowers, September; leaves appear later; perennial corm. Note: All parts of the plant are poisonous.

WOODLAND WILDLIFE

Woodland environments within the garden, however small, can be a magnet for wildlife, particularly if there is a fair proportion of native trees, shrubs and plants. In spring, healthy trees will play host to thousands of caterpillars, which provide rich pickings for bluetits and chaffinches. More unusual birds, like warblers and tree creepers which are common in oak woodlands, may be attracted to garden settings if there are large trees and dense cover; there may also be summer visitors like redstarts and pied flycatchers.

The nocturnal tawny owl nests in holes in old trees

Larger trees can accommodate hole-nesting birds such as nuthatches and spotted woodpeckers. Wood pigeons will use the fork of a sizeable trunk to make their flimsy nest and even owls might take up residence in an old, hollow tree.

Many species of butterfly will breed and feed in the woodland garden. White admirals lay their eggs on honeysuckle leaves while the caterpillars of the silver-washed fritillary feed on patches of violets. Commas, gatekeepers and speckled wood butterflies feed on ferns and grasses and can be seen basking on the plants in the dappled sunlight of a woodland edge.

The garden woodland habitat can also attract mammals, particularly if there is a pond or source of water nearby. Grey squirrels are the most frequent if not always the most popular garden visitors. Wood mice and voles will rummage about in the leaf litter looking for insects, nuts and seeds but because they are nocturnal they are rarely seen. Badgers and deer are quite frequent visitors to suburban gardens, particularly where the land backs on to woods. Badgers are nocturnal and will use a garden clearing to hunt for earthworms, insects or nuts, and can make quite a mess of the lawn in the process. Deer – like the tiny muntjac and larger roe deer – are sometimes unwelcome because they browse on young tree shoots and the foliage of garden plants like roses.

One of things we have to get used to as wild gardeners, is that some level of decay and leaf damage is inherent in a healthy garden. If we insist on sweeping up the litter and spraying our plants to combat pests then our garden has no chance of ever reproducing natural conditions. All forms of wildlife have a part to play in the woodland. Leaf litter and plant debris are home to a thriving community of insects and fungi. Snails, beetles, crickets, spiders, woodlice and earthworms all play their part in turning the fallen leaves into rich fertile humus. Splinters of wood, old logs and twigs will be attacked by fungi, causing them to rot them down into the soil. In this way the nutrients are returned to the earth and made available for the trees and plants to take them up again. Place a few logs in a shady part of the garden and watch how the wildlife increases as they start to decay.

WHERE TO SEE...
WOODLAND AND WOODLAND PLANTS

To find woods in your area, use the Ordnance Survey Landranger (1:50 000) and Pathfinder (1:25 000) maps. The Pathfinder has plenty of detail and should indicate even small woods that only cover a couple of acres. Remember, many woods are on private land and you should seek permission before exploring them. Woods owned by the National Trust, the Forestry Commission or local conservation organizations will usually be well signposted, with trails and walks open to the public. Older editions of the Ordnance Survey maps are available in county libraries (going back to the first editions from the latter half of the nineteenth century) and it is fascinating – although quite sobering – to see which local woods still exist today and which have shrunk or disappeared altogether.

Hayley Wood

One of England's most notable ancient woods, which offers a good example of spring coppice flowers and is one of the few sites left in which to see the spring flowering oxlip, Primula elatior. *It is located just off the B1046 between Longstowe and Little Gransden in Cambridgeshire, and is managed by* The Wildlife Trust for Bedfordshire, Cambridgeshire, Northamptonshire and Peterborough, Enterprise House, Maris Lane, Trumpington, Cambridgeshire CB2 2LE, telephone 01223 846363.

Warburg Reserve

Bix Bottom, Henley-on-Thames, Oxon, RG9 6BL, telephone 01491 642001. *A mixed woodland supporting a wide diversity of associated plants. It is also one of the best chalk grassland habitats in the country.*

Foxholes Reserve

A spectacular display of bluebells can be seen here in May. Foxholes Reserve is between Burford and Stow-on-the-Wold. For details contact: BBONT (Berkshire, Buckinghamshire and Oxfordshire Naturalists' Trust Limited), The Local Wildlife Trust, 3 Church Cowley Road, Oxford OX4 3JR, telephone 01865 775476.

Woodland Garden and Nursery

The Cottage Herbery, Mill House, Boraston, Nr. Tenbury Wells, Worcestershire WR15 8LZ, telephone 01584 781575. *Garden open under the National Gardens Scheme and nursery for woodland plants and herbs. Telephone for opening times before visiting.*

GENERAL CONTACTS

The Woodland Trust

Autumn Park, Dysart Road, Grantham, Lincolnshire NG31 6LL, telephone 01476 574297. *Acquires and manages woods for people and wildlife.*

The Tree Council

51 Catherine Place, London SW1E 6DY, telephone 0171-828 9928. *Runs a volunteer tree-warden scheme, enabling individuals to learn about and protect their local trees and to encourage practical projects. They also organize the annual National Tree Week (November or December) and Walk in the Woods (May), with lots of local events throughout the country.*

Chapter 2

Mea

d o w

PERHAPS NO ASPECT OF OUR COUNTRYSIDE is as emotive as the meadow. If you could take a straw poll of country lovers they would undoubtedly cite old pastures and flower-filled meadows as the habitat that seems to have disappeared most conspicuously from the landscape of their youth. Sadly, this is an accurate appraisal of the relentless changes in agricultural practices, with more arable land for wheat and barley and less grassland managed for livestock or for hay. Conservationists estimate that 97 per cent of our meadows have been lost in the past fifty years.

A traditional summer-flowering hay meadow, Hampshire

The meadow is not an entirely natural phenomenon. Old meadows contain mainly native species of plants, but the fact that the space is open and available for these grasses and flowers to colonize is because it has been cleared and managed by generations of farmers. It is because farmers don't need – or can't afford – meadows any more that they have disappeared. However, in suburban and urban gardens we have thousands of acres of grass that could be maintained as meadow. The average suburban lawn is mown short deliberately to squeeze out the meadow species in favour of rye grass mixtures. It is treated with herbicides and fertilizers, watered and cut in a vain attempt to keep the natural species from returning. The financial costs are obvious, but the long-term effects of pollution caused by the consumption of fuel and chemicals in pursuit of the perfect lawn, we can only begin to guess at. Gardens are the one place where individuals can make a difference and they represent our best chance to see the return of our meadow plants.

Grasses like Foxtail Barley (Hordeum jubatum) *are an integral part of the perennial meadow*

There is a subtle, but important, difference between pasture and meadow: pasture is land used for grazing cows, sheep or other livestock; meadow is land on which grass is allowed to go ungrazed to be cut down by the scythe in late summer for hay, which is then fed to livestock over the winter. Thus, in traditional farming practice the two types of grassland go hand in hand – a farmer needs pasture to graze his animals in the summer and meadow to produce hay for the winter. But it is the meadow that most excites our interest because of the wide range of flower species it may contain. Hay

meadows took tens, even hundreds of years to perfect and attain the best balance of species. Farmers and country people treated their meadows with respect, as a permanent fixture, not to be ploughed up for shorter-term crops.

Meadow Cranesbill (Geranium pratense) flowers in mid to late summer

A good hay meadow, rich in clover, bird's foot trefoil, hay rattle and meadow-rue, was a valuable asset and a cornerstone of the British landscape for centuries, right up until the Second World War. It was more common in counties like Lincolnshire, Nottinghamshire and Leicestershire than it was in areas where woodland was more prominent, such as the Chilterns, or in the northern counties where moorland and heath are the norm. However, most areas had some meadowland, just as they had some wood, some pasture and some arable land.

The changes have been caused partly by the huge demands placed on the land by the pressure of food production, which has led to the ploughing of meadows for arable crops, but also farming has become more specialized so that crops and livestock are rarely raised by the same farmer. Changes have also come about with the increase in silage production: there has been a switch from long-term 'leys', grassland with mixed species intended to last for generations, to short-term leys, fields planted with one type of rye grass, which can be heavily fertilized to produce earlier silage. Silage is popular with farmers because it is a more economical winter feed for cattle and is less reliant than hay on good weather. Old hay meadows and pastures have been 'improved' with fertilizers so that the grass can be cut early – in May or June as opposed to the traditional late-summer haymaking. This regime prevents most flowering species from setting seed and also disturbs the nesting meadow birds, such as skylarks and corncrakes.

Working meadows, with a mix of different grass and flower species, are now almost museum pieces, found only on land run by conservation organizations, organic farms and, of course, in gardens. Sometimes the only remnants of old meadows are the grass verges that the sprayers and cutters have missed. Despite the

general decline, tiny pockets of old grasslands have survived, like Asham and Pixey Meads in Oxfordshire, North Meadow in Wiltshire and Gowk's Bank in Cumbria, which are now protected sites. Elsewhere there are places that reflect the huge variations in landscape that can support meadow flora, from well-drained chalk downs to damp river valleys to the rocky fringes of a moorland. Often it is these marginal areas where meadow plants have survived best, because they are not on the fertile loams so attractive for food crops. In general it is more common now to see colonizations of single species, like the chalk hillside covered with pasque flowers around Easter time at Sun Hill Common in Royston or the colonies of wild daffodils in the meadows around Dymock in Gloucestershire.

THE FLOWERY MEAD

In a well-maintained acre of grass meadow there might be as many as a hundred different species. There is plenty of evidence that these flowery 'meads' (the Old English *maed* is from the verb to mow) existed well before the Norman Conquest. The word crops up in place-names such as Madehurst in Sussex, Denmead in Hampshire, Whiteoxmead in Somerset, and Shipmeadow in Suffolk and as the Anglo-Saxons were always very precise about their topographical names we can assume these all related to real meadows. Yet meadowland probably never covered the countryside in the acreages we imagine. Estimates from the time of the Domesday Survey suggest that it accounted for only about 1 or 2 per cent of the taxable land and had increased to only about 4 per cent by the thirteenth century. Nevertheless, country people have always valued and treasured their meadows: witness the people of nineteenth century Northamptonshire, who customarily dug up a piece of turf or 'greensward' full of flowers to decorate their cottages in spring and summer – not something we should contemplate today, unless it is from our own garden.

CORNFIELD WEEDS

When we first think of meadows we think more often than not of poppies, cornflowers and marigolds, those bright sunny annuals that decorate the field edges – and still occasionally the fields themselves – in summer. These flowers are not, strictly speaking, meadow flowers: they are flowers of arable land, of land that has been deliberately cultivated for 'corn' (wheat) or barley and their history seems to stretch back as far as man himself. While we think of them as our quintessential 'wild' flowers, they are in fact inextricably bound to man's exploits in the landscape and particularly to farming. Seeds of field poppies (*Papaver rhoeas*) have been found mixed with cornseed of Ancient Egypt and probably arrived in Britain with the Neolithic farmers. Later civilizations realized that they could not eliminate this vibrant 'weed' and chose instead to elevate it to a position of supernatural power. For the Romans it was sacred to their corn goddess, Ceres, and British folklore had it that to pick the flowers would bring bad luck and cause the harvest to fail.

      Cornflowers, corncockles and poppies have suffered greatly in recent years from chemical sprays. We now require our crops to be devoid of any rogue species and the cornfield weeds have all but disappeared from arable fields. However, poppies, in particular, have not been so easily silenced. The poppy seed is designed to lie dormant in the ground for years. At the first sign of disturbance, seed that was buried ten, twenty or more years before can burst into life, producing an exploding pod of thousands more seeds to scatter the earth. The poppy has become commonplace again wherever the earth is disturbed, on building sites, on the damaged remnants left by fire or bombs and

most notably on battlefields, where a shallow layer of earth covers scars that many would rather forget. Purple corncockles have been less resilient and are now rare wildflowers, occurring in East Anglia

Field poppies
(Papaver rhoeas).

and parts of Scotland. Similarly the blue cornflower occurs only intermittently in the wild and the corn marigold is declining, although not yet rare. It is perhaps a happy accident that the cornfield weeds have become such favourites of gardeners.

WATER MEADOWS

Although naturally damp grassland on the edge of rivers was always cultivated for hay, the man-made water meadow dates from around 1500, when it became more common to irrigate meadows by a complicated system of flow water and drainage channels. The idea was to flood the meadows to increase their fertility (sometimes augmented with animal and human sewage) to produce an earlier and better crop of hay. Both natural and manipulated water meadows had their own particular flora.

One of the most spectacular examples of a water meadow is the fritillary meadow at Magdalen College, Oxford, which is transformed in springtime by purple and white checked *Fritillaria meleagris*. Here, until recently, the river Cherwell flooded its banks annually from November to March. The roots are in water during the crucial growth period, but because the soil is well drained, the plant itself rarely stands in water.

The plants have adapted perfectly to this combination of natural conditions and careful management. The winter floods bring moisture to the plants and later, when the seed pods open, the seeds are scattered either by wind or by a rise in the water, which washes them further down the meadow. They are left to their own devices until late summer when the grass is cut for hay and a herd of deer is turned into the meadow to graze. The trampling of the deer helps to set the seed firmly in the meadow and ensures a good display the following spring. Even though in latter years the flood has not occurred, the water table is still high enough to keep the soil moist and to date the fritillaries have survived.

MEADOW GARDENING

There are many reasons why gardeners like the idea of having meadow in the garden. Apart from its natural beauty, it serves as a reservoir of threatened species: it supports a huge variety of insects, which will in turn support bird and mammal life and attract grassland species of butterfly. Unfortunately, to turn your dream of a flowering meadow into reality you will have to be prepared to do more than just leave the grass to grow long. The most important consideration is the site that you have in mind and whether it is well drained or slightly damp. Meadows work best in an open situation, but they can slope down to a stream or a pond, or extend up to the edge of a shrub border or woodland. They might be carved out of an existing lawn or set in an area that was previously uncultivated. They tend to work best away from formal flower borders, where the garden can take on a more relaxed feel, perhaps as part of the gradation from cultivated garden to the landscape beyond.

CONVERTING A LAWN TO MEADOW

Some people are not prepared to get rid of their lawn completely and others simply do not have the room to give over all the lawn area to meadow flowers. Areas of short grass are very useful if you have children or pets or if you simply want a usable area of grass. Meadows, once planted, are not very usable, although it's quite simple to mow paths through the long grass for access. The first step towards converting a lawn to meadow is to define the areas you want to keep as short grass by mowing these closely, leaving the others to grow longer. Another alternative would be to raise the mower cutting-height to 5 cm (2 in) or more. This will allow daisies, clover and speedwell to flourish and will give a more natural appearance than grass cut at 2.5 cm (1 in).

If you are ready to take the plunge and convert a lawn into a full-blown wildflower meadow then the next most important consideration is the fertility of the area. If the lawn is already patchy and weedy, then the chances are that fertility is low and its condition is perfect for introducing wildflowers. If the grass is green and lush then the fertility is probably too high and you will need to strip off the turf and some of the topsoil, and start the meadow from scratch. Most lawns have a high percentage of rye grass, which is tough and tends to swamp any other species. Other grasses, however, such as quaking grass and oat grass, are finer, more delicate species that should be included in a wildflower meadow. We should not be aiming to eradicate all grasses and the best meadows are a delicate balance of different flowers and grass species.

SEED SOWING IN EXISTING GRASS

A relatively simple way to start a meadow is to sow seed in the existing grass in autumn. This should only be attempted where the grass is already poor and patchy.

◆ Rake the lawn or grass thoroughly with a metal rake to remove all the dead grass, moss, stones and fallen leaves.

◆ Mow the grass as normal, removing all the clippings. Rake the grass hard again, so that the top surface of the soil is disturbed slightly.

◆ Water the area thoroughly and then sow a meadow-flower seed mixture at the seed merchant's recommended rate. This is usually 4 gm per square metre but can vary.

◆ Leave the area undisturbed until the following spring. Cut the grass down when it is over 10 cm (4 in) high – removing all the cuttings. It is best to use a rotary mower or a Strimmer for a cutting height of between 5 and 10 cm (2–4 in). A scythe is the best tool for cutting down long grass, but can be dangerous if not used by an experienced person. Garden shears will do for a small area.

◆ Continue to cut each time the height gets much over 10 cm in the first season. This will give the new flower seedlings a chance to develop, and will keep weeds under control. In the second season, it will not need to be cut as often, perhaps just twice during the season.

Lupins (Lupinus polyphyllus) *are sometimes grown as a fodder crop, creating colourful fields like this one in Hampshire*

PLANTING IN EXISTING GRASS

Early autumn is also a good time to introduce pot-grown wildflowers into a lawn or patch of grass. These have the advantage over seed in that you can choose exactly the flowers that you want. The root systems will already be fairly well developed, which means they will have a head start against the invasive rye grass.

◆ Give the lawn or grass a final close mowing at the end of the season and water it well.

◆ Set the wildflower plants in groups or drifts for a natural effect. Clear the turf off the areas you are going to plant to give them a better chance of establishment.

◆ Put in each plant approximately 20–30 cm (8–12 in) from its neighbour, using a bulb planter or trowel to remove a plug of earth. Firm the soil down well and water in.

◆ In the first year after planting follow the same cutting regime as above.

SOWING A MEADOW FROM SCRATCH

Undoubtedly the best way to achieve a successful wildflower meadow is to prepare a bare earth site and sow the seeds in early autumn. The area needs to be prepared in the same way as for a conventional lawn – it should be dug over to remove any perennial weeds and large stones and then sieved and raked to a fine, level tilth. If you have a really persistent problem with weeds like ground elder or couch grass, it is best to choose another site as they will always recur and threaten the meadow. Assess the site and choose a seed mixture designed for your particular conditions, that is for chalky, sandy or clay soil or for particularly damp soil – good wildflower seed merchants offer a choice of mixtures. If in doubt go for a standard meadow mixture: most consist of 20 per cent flowers and 80 per cent grasses but the species contained within them will vary (see p.57).

◆ Prepare the ground by raking and levelling, and water thoroughly using a hose with a sprinkler fitting or a watering can with a rose. Make sure that the ground is well soaked.

◆ Mix the seed with silver sand to make it easier to sow.

◆ To sow the seed and make sure the ground is covered evenly, walk the plot in one direction (that is, up and down), sowing thinly (at half the recommended rate) and then sow it again in the opposite direction (that is, across).

◆ After sowing lightly tread over the plot so that the seeds are in good contact with the earth. Don't bury them as this can reduce germination. Mark the edges of the area with pea sticks or short canes and cover with fruit netting if birds are likely to be a problem. This is a good idea anyway, as it marks out the area and prevents anyone walking on it.

◆ In the first spring and summer after sowing follow the same cutting regime as for the other methods above.

SOWING CORNFIELD FLOWERS

The alternative to a traditional meadow as described above is an annual meadow of cornfield flowers – poppies, marigolds and so on. Although this is what many people think of as a meadow it is actually a fairly short-term aspect of the wild garden. Cornfield flowers thrive on land that is cultivated every year, and to ensure a good display of colour, the ground will need to be dug or forked over and re-sown each spring. There are several ways of introducing this kind of flowering habitat. If you want to see a colourful display from early summer onwards, sow the annual seeds in spring on any patch of bare, disturbed soil. Most gardens have an area that is useless for conventional plants – such as the site of the autumn bonfire, a stony patch of earth that has never been cultivated, the ground left when the builders have all but removed their rubble, all are ideal for the

A typical meadow includes ox-eye daisies, yarrow, clover and grasses

cornfield annuals. They will self-seed, but it is rare for an equally good display to occur in the same place in the second year. The way to encourage the fallen seeds to germinate is to rake or dig over the area again in the spring. This disturbs the soil, bringing some seeds to the surface and covering others with soil – perfect conditions for germination.

Cornflowers and yellow chamomile (Anthemis tinctoria)

Another way to use the cornfield annuals is to take a tip from the professional meadow sowers, who often use poppies, corn marigolds and cornflowers as 'nursing' plants for the perennial meadow flowers. By mixing annual cornfield seeds in with the traditional meadow mixture, the annuals germinate in the first summer to provide cover for the slower-growing perennial plants. They also take the place of any weeds or more aggressive grasses, giving the real meadow plants a chance to establish and thrive. It should state clearly on the seed packet whether or not annual flowers are included. Often when gardeners sow these meadow mixtures, they are delighted with the colourful poppies of the first year but assume when they don't return the second year that their meadow is a failure. If you do have annuals in your mix and want to see them flower again, leave the grass uncut until late summer when the seeds will have ripened and fallen. Otherwise, enjoy the colourful show but accept that a traditional hay meadow does not contain many of these bright annual flowers: it has a gentler beauty of its own.

MEADOW MANAGEMENT

The traditional way of managing hay meadows was to cut them down in late summer to remove the hay and then to turn cattle and other livestock in to graze in the autumn before they were brought indoors for the winter. Once a meadow is established, it can be managed on the same principles: one cut per year in late summer, followed by occasional cuts during the autumn and winter. Each meadow is different and this is not a hard and fast regime. If the meadow has a high proportion of spring flowers, such as cowslips and buttercups, you can cut it when these are over in early summer. If the main species are summer-flowering, such as scabious and knapweed, then it is best to leave the cutting until these have set seed. If the meadow is looking good, with a nice balance of flowers and native grasses, then this once or twice a year routine works well. However, if the lawn grasses are still dominant, it is best to keep cutting to maintain a height of around 10 cm (4 in) or the flowers will be swamped. After cutting down the meadow, leave the 'hay' where it has fallen for a day or two to dry out; this makes it easier to remove. Then, rake it off and use it for animals or add it to the compost heap. Meadows take a few years to establish, but once the mix of species in the turf has stabilized, this regime of once or twice yearly cutting will keep it flowering for hundreds of years.

TYPICAL MEADOW
SEED MIXTURE

GRASSES 80%
Bent (*Agrostis castellana*) 10%
Crested Dogtail (*Cynosurus cristatus*) 40%
Fescue (*Festuca rubra*) 10%
Meadow Barley (*Hordeum secalinum*) 5%
Quaking Grass (*Briza media*) 15%

FLOWERS 20%
Cowslip (*Primula veris*)
Lady's Bedstraw (*Galium verum*)
Lesser Knapweed (*Centaurea nigra*)
Musk Mallow (*Malva moschata*)
Ox-Eye Daisy (*Leucanthemum vulgare*)
Red Clover (*Trifolium pratense*)
Ribwort Plantain (*Plantago lanceolata*)
Self-heal (*Prunella vulgaris*)
Sorrel (*Rumex acetosa*)
Yarrow (*Achillea millefolium*)
Yellow Rattle (*Rhinanthus minor*)

NEW PERENNIAL MEADOW

In the last few years a new approach to planting has emerged that is somewhere between the herbaceous border and the traditional hay meadow, known as the 'perennial meadow'.

Garden perennials are planted in drifts to create a 'meadow' effect

It is not a meadow in the wild sense but a way of using cultivated perennial plants to create a more natural effect. As with other types of wild gardening, the aim is to choose plants that will be happy in their situation and will then need no feeding or watering and only a minimum of weeding. The idea is to create a garden that takes care of itself and needs little or no intervention from the gardener.

It is an idea that has become popular in Europe, particularly in Germany and Holland where the idea has spread to both private gardens and public parks. Nurseries have been developing cultivars and hybrids that are closer to their natural parents in looks – that is, they have a more wild appearance – but are sturdy and well behaved in a garden setting. These plants work hard for their living, either with long-lasting flowers, interesting seed-heads, good foliage or a compact shape that doesn't need staking. All are selected because they will rarely need the amounts of tender loving care that we usually lavish on herbaceous borders. The plants selected are mainly singles, tend to be fairly small in stature and are resistant to pests and diseases.

The Americans have also adopted meadow gardening, extending the idea to include native prairie species, like blue camassias, yellow solidagos and bright orange

asclepias. Once the gardener has absorbed the principles behind the perennial meadow the choice of species from all over the world is endless.

The perennial meadow uses a combination of perennials, bulbs, grasses and herbs to produce a garden that has more structure than a wild meadow but less than the conventional border. The plants are interwoven in waves or drifts rather than clumps to give an impression of flowing movement. Not all the plants are herbaceous, so the meadow can look just as good in autumn and winter as it does in summer, with grasses and seed heads providing interest after the flowers have gone.

PLANTING WITH PERENNIALS

As with the wildflower meadow, preparation is the key to success. First, the area to be planted should be weeded and dug over. High fertility is not important and, in fact, if the ground is too rich, the plants will put on too much lush growth and become floppy and difficult to manage, spoiling the effect. This kind of planting is ideal for ordinary soils that have not been heavily fertilized. If the soil is particularly light (for example, pure sand) or very heavy (for example, sticky clay) then it is worth working in some organic matter such as leaf mould or garden compost to make it more friable. The area could be an existing border – although it will look better if it is curved rather than rectangular – or it could replace an existing lawn or hard landscaping. If you need to plant on a former vegetable patch that has been heavily fed, dig in some sand to reduce the fertility.

Young perennials should be planted in autumn when the soil is moist and still warm. They can also be planted in spring, although they may not be well established by the first summer. New plants should be watered well before and after planting. Until the plants fill out, the bare earth around them can be covered with a mulch of gravel, compost or bark. This will help to suppress weeds and conserve water in the early stages of growth.

One of the key differences between this kind of planting and the old-fashioned border is that the plants should not look regimented. It is not necessary to put tall plants at the back and low growers at the front. Intersperse plants of different heights and shapes to give an undulating effect. You can also sow some self-seeding annual flowers, such as California poppies, between the main plants, particularly in the first year or so, to give an established look.

LOOKING AFTER THE PERENNIAL MEADOW

The whole point of a perennial meadow is that it should look after itself, particularly once it has become established. If the plants are not continually fed, they will not put on as much lush foliage and therefore will not be as prone to pest attack and disease. The dense planting will naturally keep weeds at bay and conserve moisture in the soil. Stems and seed heads should be left on the plants as long as possible, not only because they are attractive but also because they are useful to seed-feeding birds like finches, and for overwintering insects. As each species starts to look too untidy, dead stems and leaves can be cut back with secateurs, but this should be something you do periodically from late summer to early spring, rather than cutting down the whole meadow at once. You will need to lift and divide some of the plants once they start to flower poorly or to outgrow their space, but this is not likely to be for four or five years. Self-seeding annuals can be weeded out if they threaten the balance of the display, but otherwise can be left to give a more natural look.

PERENNIAL MEADOW PLANTS

	HEIGHT X SPREAD
Achillea filipendulina 'Cloth of Gold'	90 cm (3 ft) x 60 cm (2 ft)
Long, mid-green leaves; large golden yellow flower-heads, July to September	
Achillea 'Moonshine'	90 cm (3 ft) x 60 cm (2 ft)
. *Long, mid-green leaves; pale yellow flower-heads, July to September*	
Euphorbia characias 'Blue Hills'	90 cm (3 ft) x 90 cm (3 ft)
Pale grey-green leaves; greenish-purple flowers, April/May; evergreen. Note: Euphorbia sap can cause skin irritations.	
California Tree Poppy (*Romneya coulteri*)	2 m (6 ft) x 2 m (6 ft)
Lobed, grey-green leaves; white poppy-like flowers, July to October; shrubby perennial	

Scabious (*Scabiosa columbaria* var. *ochroleuca*)   30 cm (12 in) x 30 cm (12 in)
Grey-green leaves; lilac flower-heads, June to August; evergreen

Foxtail Lily (*Eremurus* x *isabellinus* Shelford Hybrids)   1.2 m (4 ft) x 1 m (3 ft)
Long (60 cm/ 2ft) narrow leaves; towering flower spikes in pastel colours,
May/June

Golden Rod (*Solidago* 'Cloth of Gold')   45 cm (18 in) x 25 cm (10 in)
Lance-shaped leaves; bright yellow flower stems, August/September

Penstemon (*Penstemon* 'Garnet')   60 cm (24 in) x 30 cm (12 in)
Lance-shaped leaves; deep red tubular flowers, June to September; hardy

Geranium (*Geranium versicolor*)   30 cm (12 in) x 30 cm (12 in)
Shiny green leaves with reddish markings; white flowers with purple veins, May
to September; evergreen

SELF-SEEDING MEADOW ANNUALS

California Poppies (*Eschscholzia californica*)   35 cm (14 in) x 23 cm (9 in)
Finely divided, blue-grey foliage; yellow or orange poppy-like flowers, June to
October;

Love-in-a-Mist (*Nigella damascena*)   50 cm (20 in) x 25 cm (10 in)
Finely divided, green foliage; blue flowers, June/July; attractive seed-heads

Opium Poppy (*Papaver somniferum*)   60 cm (24 in) x 45 cm (18 in)
Grey-green leaves; white, pink or purple flowers, June/July; attractive grey-
green seed pods. Note: The sap of the plant is toxic, although the seeds are safe.

BULBS

Camassia (*Camassia quamash*)   60 cm (24 in) x 30 cm (12 in)
Long, linear leaves; violet blue flower spikes, May/June

Camassia (*Camassia leichtlinii*)   1 m (3 ft) x 30 cm (1 ft)
Narrow, erect leaves; large purple flower spikes, May/June; 'Alba' is white form

Allium (*Allium sphaerocephalon*)   60 cm (2 ft) x 30 cm (1 ft)
Linear, hollow leaves; reddish flower heads, July/August; good for bees

GRASSES

Foxtail Barley (*Hordeum jubatum*)   60 cm (24 in) x 30 cm (12 in)
Light green leaves; pink or buff-coloured bristles, June/July

Stipa calamagrostis   75 cm (30 in) x 1.2 m (4 ft)
Narrow, green leaves; feathery, waving flower-heads, June to October

Quaking Grass (*Briza media*)   60 cm (24 in) x 30 cm (12 in)
Mid-green leaves; pale green spikes turn straw coloured, June to August

HERBS

Golden Marjoram (*Origanum vulgare* 'Aureum')   30 cm (12 in) x 60 cm (24 in)
Aromatic golden leaves; spreading; inconspicuous purple flowers,
August/September

Bronze Fennel (*Foeniculum vulgare* 'Purpureum')   2 m (6 ft) x 60 cm (2 ft)
Bronze feathery foliage; yellow flowers, July; aromatic seeds

Borage (*Borago officinalis*)   60 cm (2 ft) x 30 cm (1 ft)
Coarse, hairy leaves; blue, star-shaped flowers, June to September; self-seeding
annual

MEADOW PLANTS

Wildflower meadow plants are at their best in spring and summer and all the planting is geared towards giving a good display from April until the meadow is cut in August. The typical old hay meadow might be filled with buttercups and cowslips in spring, followed by ox-eye daisies, meadow cranesbill, knapweeds and orchids in the summer. The grasses are as important as the flowers in creating a haze of colour, particularly as they mature towards the end of the season and produce flower-heads and spikes which, if less conspicuous than true flowers, are just as

RIGHT: Meadow grasses and flowers in an informal border
BELOW: Leucanthemum vulgare (Ox-eye Daisy)

attractive. Meadow barley (*Hordeum secalinum*) has prolific fawn flower-heads; yellow oat grass (*Tisetum flavescens*) produces a golden shining haze, Yorkshire fog (*Holcus lanatus*), as its common name suggests, has a downy flower-head that gives the meadow a misty appearance and the flowers of the red fescue (*Festuca rubra*) have a purplish tinge, all of which add variation and interest to the meadow.

BUTTERCUPS AND DAISIES

The first flowers we associate with spring meadows and pastures are buttercups and daisies, although they can stay in bloom from April right through to September. The meadow buttercup (*Ranunculus acris*) is found in many old meadows and grazing pastures, although for it to thrive, the soil needs to be at least moist if not damp. It has quite tall stems with the characteristic buttery yellow flowers but the leaves are poisonous and livestock avoid it, which is probably why it is so abundant in some fields. If your soil is dry an alternative is the bulbous buttercup (*R. bulbosus*), a shorter plant that thrives on well-drained chalk or acid soils.

Buttercups can hold their own in long grass, but daisies (*Bellis perennis*) are more commonly found on the shorter turf of grazed pasture or cropped verges. A lawn that is not treated with herbicides or fertilizers or mowed too closely will often produce a carpet of daisies and for some wildflower gardeners this is as far as they want to go in the meadow stakes. Daisies are one of those flowers that seem so abundant, but look around the average estate of suburban gardens and they have all but vanished from the acres of green lawns. They have been devalued to the level of a weed, when they were once prized as a medicinal herb for treating cuts and wounds, and as Chaucer's favourite flower in the Prologue to the *Canterbury Tales*. The north of England and Scottish name for the daisy is 'eye of day', a direct translation of the Anglo-Saxon 'day's eye' – clearly because the petals open in the morning and close at dusk.

A spring meadow should also include cowslips (*Primula veris*), not the most elegant of names as it is in fact a polite form of cow 'slop' or dung. Genteel sensibilities aside, the name is a fair clue to its favoured habitat: cattle pastures and meadows. In fact, it grows in a range of grassy environments, but it prefers the drier, chalkier soils of the open field (compare its woodland cousins the primrose and oxlip, p.32) although, of course, it has no objection to a generous dose of organic manure. It is a true spring flower, appearing only in April and May, so it can safely be grown in a garden meadow that will be cut down in early summer. It could make a good companion for meadow saxifrage (*Saxifraga granulata*), a dainty white plant sometimes grown in borders but which looks far more at home among the longer grasses of a meadow.

From late spring onwards, one of the most dominant species in the meadow is the white and yellow ox-eye daisy (*Leucanthemum vulgare*). These tall perennial flowers with their golden centres and rays of dazzling white petals are easy to establish from seed or as pot-plants and should give a good show by the second year at the latest. They tolerate a range of soil conditions from moist to dry, and should be perfectly at home on all but the most acid soils. The ox-eye daisy is not a new plant in gardens and its range of country names – dog daisy, moon daisy and marguerite – are tribute to its having been well known to cottage gardeners for centuries. It can be grown as a border plant, although in good soil it soon becomes invasive and needs to be dug up and divided regularly. It was probably from this plant that the gardener first acquired a taste for large daisy-type flowers, which led to the breeding of hybrids, the most famous of which, the Shasta daisy (*Leucanthemum* x *superbum*) is available in a range of double and semi-double flowered cultivars for the herbaceous border.

THE SUMMER MEADOW

Old hay meadows almost always included yellow rattle (*Rhinanthus minor*), a low-growing annual mainly distinguished by the seed pods, which rattle in the wind when they are ripe. When the hay was cut they must have made quite a noise, hence the local names hay rattle, baby's rattle and rattlebags. It is neither a rare nor a particularly attractive plant, but one without which a meadow would simply not be a true meadow. It is a useful parasite in that its roots draw their nourishment from nearby grass roots, stunting the grass and improving its own and other wildflowers' chances of survival. Another typical meadow flower is great burnet (*Sanguisorba officinalis*), with densely packed crimson flower-heads floating above tall slender stalks. It is a perennial plant that prefers damp ground. For

drier meadows, particularly on chalk or limestone soils, the smaller salad burnet (*Sanguisorba minor*) is a better choice and it has the added advantage that the young leaves are edible and can be used in salads. Both will be in flower from June to August.

A meadow is more than the sum of its parts: when we take some of its plants individually they are not species that gardeners would ever want to grow in anything other than a meadow habitat. Red clover (*Trifolium pratense*), bird's foot trefoil (*Lotus corniculatus*) and lady's bedstraw (*Galium verum*) are all vital constituents of the summer meadow but fairly flimsy plants in their own right. Yet if we take the time to get to know them, they all have at least one outstanding quality. The golden yellow flowers of lady's bedstraw are fragrant, attractive to insects, and were traditionally dried and used to stuff mattresses and as a strewing herb in the house. Bird's foot trefoil is attractive to bumble bees and an important butterfly food plant. The two-tone flowers are instantly recognizable and have given rise to some interesting local names, including butter-and-eggs, shoes-and-stockings and eggs-and-bacon. Red clover was important for livestock, but children also love to pick off the flowers and suck the bases for nectar – as, of course, do bees, in a roundabout way.

Some of the most visible meadow flowers appear late in the season. The knapweeds are the perennial relatives of the cornflowers and have the same fringed flower heads. The common knapweed (*Centaurea nigra*) is the most frequently seen species in July and August, with its thistle-like purple flowers measuring about 2.5 cm (1 in) across. More spectacular is the greater knapweed (*Centaurea scabiosa*), with larger flowers and longer, more tufted petals. When the flower-heads have finished, finches descend upon the seed-heads. Neither plant can be described as delicate, and for this quality we must look to the pin-cushion pale lilac flowers of the field scabious (*Knautia arvensis*), which also flowers in late summer and is attractive to bees and butterflies.

CORNFIELD FLOWERS

Top: *Wild teasel*
(Dipsacus fullonum)

Left: *Greater knapweed*
(Centaura scabiosa)

A wild garden would not be complete without poppies, cornflowers and marigolds, whether the original field species or their hundreds of garden relatives. Wild poppies (*Papaver rhoeas*) only really look at home in a meadow or rough patch of ground (see p. 50) but other poppies can find a natural and happy setting in the garden. The annual Shirley poppies would probably be the wild gardener's second choice: named after the

Midlands home town of the Reverend Wilkes, who raised the strain in 1880 from a rogue red and white poppy he found growing in a local field, they are delicate, single flowers in colours ranging from rose pink to pure white. They have no black blotch at the base like the field poppies, but are otherwise quite similar and can be grown in a meadow situation or in a sunny, annual bed without grasses. The lilac or purple opium poppy (*P. somniferum*) is a native of Eastern Europe and Asia, but can be found growing naturalized on wasteland and by roadsides throughout Britain. It is also an annual, but easy to tell apart from the other poppies because the flowers are much larger – up to 15 cm (6 in) across – and the dark blotch on the petals is pronounced. Opium poppies grow well in Britain but our summers are not hot enough for them to produce the right chemicals for heroin and morphine, for which they are grown in other countries. This poppy has edible seeds, which are used to decorate bread and cakes. Gardeners with herbaceous borders will already be familiar with the oriental poppy (*P. orientale*), which forms huge, colourful clumps and is an essential ingredient if you want to create a more permanent but natural planting scheme (see New Perennial Meadow, p. 58).

Annual cornflower
(Centaura cyanus)

The annual cornflower (*Centaurea cyanus*), with its violet-blue flowers, is now rare in the wild and all the more reason for including it in a meadow or annual border. Like all the *Centaurea* genus, which includes knapweeds and some thistles, it is happiest on open, well-drained ground with low fertility, which has preferably undergone some disturbance. It is a surprisingly tall plant, reaching up to 1 m (3 ft) high, although some garden cultivars have been bred to stay more compact. Again, in more traditional gardens the perennial cornflower (*C. montana*) has found favour as a clump-forming plant with a number of pretty pink and white garden forms.

Poppies and cornflowers are natural companions to the magenta-flowered corncockle (*Agrostemma githago*), another tall, slender plant that looks at its best in waving grass or crowded together with other summer annuals. It is a Mediterranean native – which gives a clue to the dry, sunny conditions it likes best – but until recently was common in cornfields and on road verges. Now it is confined to a few local spots where it has naturalized itself, in East Anglia and Scotland, though perhaps we should not mourn its demise in the countryside as Britain was not its first home. The corn chamomile (*Anthemis arvensis*), with its fragrant yellow and white flowers, can still be seen on the edges of arable fields and can easily be included in an annual flower patch along with yellow corn marigolds (*Chrysanthemum segetum*), both of which are lightly scented.

BULBS AND TUBERS FOR A DAMP MEADOW

Damp grassland, or a soggy lawn, offers the gardener the chance to grow some of the most beautiful wildflowers, particularly those that appear in late spring. The easiest way to plant up a damp lawn is simply to introduce one species of bulbous plant, such as the snake's head fritillary, leave the grass long until after the plants have set seed and then cut it normally through the rest of the year. This is known as naturalizing and the plants should self-seed and spread without any further interference. The purple and white chequered native *Fritillaria meleagris* is protected in the wild, but the bulbs and seeds are widely available from nurseries. Plant the bulbs 10–15 cm (4–6 in) deep in autumn in a random formation and cover them with soil or turf. Resist the temptation to mow the grass until mid- to late summer when all the seed will have dropped. Then mow the grass short – an occasional rolling, with a lawn roller, will ensure that the seed is set well into the soil. Keep mowing until the cold weather stops the growth and there should be a good display next spring. A similar regime can be adopted for the wild daffodil (*Narcissus pseudonarcissus*), bulbs of which can be bought from wildflower specialists. This is a much more delicate plant than the garden daffodils and it looks at its best growing in longish grass. Plant the bulbs 8 cm (3 in) deep in autumn and leave the grass to grow long until midsummer. If the bulbs fail it may be because the ground dries out too much in summer.

Many gardeners mistakenly believe that orchids have no part in a wild garden, or that if they do, they are terribly difficult to grow. Yet around fifty species are native to or naturalized in Britain, growing unaided in a huge range of habitats from woodlands and marshlands to moorland and field. The easiest orchid to grow in the garden meadow is the common spotted orchid (*Dactylorhiza fuchsii*), which has beautiful pink flower spikes and will form large colonies once established. The Dactylorhiza orchids are now fairly widely available from nurseries and are easy to grow from tubers planted in the autumn. They need a moist soil and naturalize well in damp grass.

FLOWERS FOR A DAMP MEADOW

	HEIGHT
Meadow Buttercup (*Ranunculus acris*)	60 cm (2 ft)
Deeply divided basal leaves; small golden yellow flowers, April to September; perennial	
Lady's Smock/Cuckoo Flower (*Cardamine pratensis*)	45 cm (18 in)
Numerous narrow leaflets; pale lilac-pink flowers, April to June; spreading perennial	
Ragged Robin (*Lychnis flos-cuculi*)	60 cm (2 ft)
Pointed, deep green leaves; rose pink, shaggy flowers, May to July; perennial	
Wild Daffodil (*Narcissus pseudonarcissus*)	30 cm (12 in)
Narrow, strap-shaped leaves; pale yellow trumpets, March/April; bulb	
Fritillary (*Fritillaria meleagris*)	23 cm (9 in)
Linear, grey-green leaves; purple and white checked lanterns, April/May; bulb	

Jacob's Ladder (*Polemonium caeruleum*) 60 cm (2 ft)
  Narrow leaflets; blue flower clusters, May to July; perennial

Meadowsweet (*Filipendula ulmaria*) 90 cm (3 ft)
  Dark green lobed leaves; fragrant cream flowers, June to September; perennial

Common Spotted Orchid (*Dactylorhiza fuchsii*) 45 cm (18 in)
  Linear spotted leaves; pink flower spikes, June/July; tuber

Greater Burnet (*Sanguisorba officinalis*) 30–60 cm (12–24 in)
  Oval, toothed leaves, grey underneath; crimson oval flower-heads, June to August; perennial

SPRING MEADOW FLOWERS

Daisy (*Bellis perennis*) 10 cm (4 in)
  Basal rosette of leaves; yellow and white flowers, April to August; perennial

Cowslip (*Primula veris*) 23 cm (9 in)
  Veined oblong leaves; yellow drooping flowers, April/May; perennial

Meadow Saxifrage (*Saxifraga granulata*) 30 cm (12 in)
  Lobed kidney-shaped leaves; white flower clusters, April to June; perennial

Sorrel (*Rumex acetosa*) 30–45 cm (12–18 in)
  Arrow-shaped leaves; inconspicuous pink flower spikes, May/June; perennial

Salad Burnet (*Sanguisorba minor*) 15–30 cm (6–12 in)
  Rounded, toothed leaflets; round, pinkish flower heads, May to August; perennial

Germander Speedwell (*Veronica chamaedrys*) 10 cm (4 in)
  Dark green toothed leaves; small bright blue flowers, white centre, March to June; spreading perennial

Bulbous Buttercup (*Ranunculus bulbosus*) 30 cm (12 in)
  Lobed basal leaves; small bright yellow flowers, March to July; perennial

SUMMER MEADOW FLOWERS

Red Clover (*Trifolium pratense*) 15 cm (6 in)
  Oval leaves; reddish purple flowers, May to September; perennial

Meadow Cranesbill (*Geranium pratense*) 60 cm (2 ft)
  Deeply divided leaves; bright violet flowers, June to September; perennial

Ox-eye Daisy (*Leucanthemum vulgare*) 60 cm (2 ft)
  Dark green toothed leaves; white flowers with yellow disc, May to August; perennial

Common Knapweed (*Centaurea nigra*) 60 cm (2 ft)
  Elliptical leaves; fringed, thistle-like, purple flower-heads, June to September; perennial

Greater Knapweed (*Centaurea scabiosa*) 60 cm (2 ft)
  Linear, lobed leaves; large purple fringed flower heads, June to September; perennial

Bird's Foot Trefoil (*Lotus corniculatus*) 15 cm (6 in)
  Oval, clover-like leaves; orangey-yellow flowers, June to September; sprawling perennial

Yarrow (*Achillea millefolium*) 30 cm (12 in)
  Feathery, grey-green leaves; dense flower-heads, white, occasional pink, June to September; perennial

Yellow Rattle (*Rhinanthus minor*) 10–30 cm (4–12 in)
  Toothed, nettle-like leaves; pale yellow flowers, June to September; perennial

MEADOW WILDLIFE

With so little meadowland remaining in Britain, it goes without saying that much of the wildlife we associate with meadows has disappeared too. Skylarks are one of the best-known casualties of the chemical agricultural revolution, along with corn buntings and English partridges, none of which we are likely to attract into gardens. Nevertheless, the range of flowers and grasses in a wild meadow will attract and support a range of insects and butterflies that would not be seen in gardens with conventional rye-grass lawns. The long grass provides hiding places for caterpillars, larvae and invertebrates while the flowers provide nectar for adult butterflies, bees, moths and other garden insects. You might also find grasshoppers, ladybirds, spiders, and certainly one or two field or bank voles. These are the hidden wildlife of the meadow that help to make it a more vibrant and complete environment.

Hoverflies feed on meadow flowers and help to control garden aphids

Butterfly larvae have fairly specific food requirements. Species like the common blue and the dingy skipper have a preference for bird's foot trefoil (*Lotus corniculatus*), the small copper feeds on sorrel (*Rumex acetosa*) while the orange tip and the green-veined white butterflies feed on the lady's smock (*Cardamine pratense*). The soft meadow grasses provide food for the meadow brown, the gatekeeper, the small heath, the small skipper and the ringlet. Adult butterflies are not as dependent on particular plants as their young, but they will all feed on the nectar provided by a good flowering meadow. A spring meadow will provide nectar for any butterflies that emerge early and later flushes of flowers like the knapweed, field scabious and yarrow will do the same for the second and third broods. A garden sometimes scores over a natural environment in that the habitats are telescoped closer together. This means that woodland-edge species like the Duke of Burgundy fritillary can use both the woodland and the meadow habitats – its caterpillar food plants are primroses, found in the damper shadier parts of the woodland, and cowslips, found in the drier open meadow.

With the increased numbers of insects in the meadow, the bird population will naturally use the area as a feeding ground. Swallows and swifts may swoop over in their busy breeding months and you may occasionally see a green woodpecker low over the ground, with its characteristic undulating flight and raucous call. The green woodpecker is a much larger bird than the black-and-white great and lesser spotted woodpeckers of woodlands, and it spends much more time on the ground, feeding on insects. In late summer the seed-heads of the meadow grasses will be a magnet to small seed-eating birds, like chaffinches, greenfinches, linnets and tits.

WHERE TO SEE...
MEADOWS AND MEADOW PLANTS

The sad truth is, you have search hard to find a traditional hay meadow. Some forward-thinking farmers and conservation organizations are trying to redress the balance. Poppies and other cornfield annuals are more likely to be seen on road verges than in fields, and gardens have become the last refuge of many perennial meadow flowers.

MEADOWS

Courtyard Farm
Ringstead, Hunstanton, Norfolk PE36 5LQ, telephone 01485 525212.
A commercial farm taking a positive approach to farming and conservation. There are areas of chalk grassland and woodland, and in June/July some fields are planted with cornfield annuals. The farm itself is not open to the public but footpaths are well signposted and visitors are urged to stick closely to them. A leaflet detailing the footpaths is available either from the above address or from the car park next to the farm.

Magdalen College
High Street, Oxford OX1 4AU, telephone 01865 276001.
In April, sheets of Fritillaria meleagris *can be seen in the water meadow.*

Ducklington, Oxfordshire
Every year on the last Sunday in April this village hosts a Fritillary Sunday. The meadow and church are open to the public, and there are plant stalls and cream teas.

Cricklade, Gloucestershire
English Nature's meadow at Cricklade is a National Nature Reserve and internationally important for its rich flora. It supports the largest population of Fritillaria meleagris *in Britain and comprises over a hundred acres of traditionally managed hay meadow. The fritillaries can be seen in April, followed by a wide variety of meadow plants in June and July.*

Gowk Bank Meadow, Cumbria
English Nature, Juniper House, Murley Moss, Oxenholme Road, Kendal LA9 7RL, telephone 01539 792800.
Contact Terry Wells for details of Gowk Bank and other species-rich meadows in the area. For meadows in other parts of the country, contact English Nature's main office (see addresses p. x).

MEADOW PLANTS

Emorsgate Seeds
Limes Farm, Tilney All Saints, King's Lynn, Norfolk PE34 4RT, telephone 01553 829028.
Producers and suppliers of British wildflower seed. Advice given on sowing and on choosing the right meadow mixtures for different soils and situations.

British Wild Flower Plants
23 Yarmouth Road, Ormesby St Margaret, Gt Yarmouth NR29 3QE, telephone 01493 730244.
Contact Linda Laxton. Mail-order nursery growing over four hundred species of native wildflowers including many grasses, sedges and rushes not often available elsewhere.

Glebe Cottage Plants
Pixie Lane, Warkleigh, Umberleigh, Devon, EX 37 9DH.
Extensive collection of plants for different situations

Chapter 3

Wetl

and

IN THE WILD OR IN THE GARDEN, water has an air of permanence. The rains fill the streams, the streams rush down to the rivers and the rivers flow to the sea, where the cycle starts again. Ponds, lakes, marshes, broads and fens entrance us with their 'wildness'. As you stand by a stream or river, the water gives out a sense of antiquity – of 'going on for ever'.

What is it about wetlands that makes them so magical? Lichen and mosses clinging to rocks by the side of a fast-flowing stream; wading birds picking their harvest of lugworms and snails from the mud flats of a tidal estuary; huge colourful dragonflies darting across the village pond; rare orchids clinging to survival in freshwater marshes – these are the pictures of wetland that are so enduring and so attractive. Yet these are exactly the landscapes that are under threat from human carelessness.

The English Lake District and the Norfolk Broads are, perhaps, the two best examples of how we accord to our wetlands a magical, almost mythical status and then descend on them in droves to do more damage than we can ever imagine. Over much of the countryside, modern field drainage systems have literally sucked the land dry, leaving fewer and fewer wet or marshy areas for the thousands of species that depend upon them. Species like the great crested newt have disappeared from many areas and even the common frog is a rarity in some parts of the country. Luckily there are still places that are less accessible to tourism, agriculture or industrial development, such as the

Early morning light,
Fast Rabbit Farm, Devon

mountain streams that course the higher reaches of the Scottish mountain ranges, and the wet heaths on the westernmost reaches of coastal Wales. In more accessible areas there are signs now that people are recognizing the value of water, in well cared-for village ponds, for example, and rivers free of pollution. Farmers are taking steps to keep clean and usable the water on their land. In urban areas, former gravel-pits and industrial sites are being turned into ponds and marsh. And it is in these wetlands – in our own neighbourhoods and in our own gardens – that we can make a difference. Garden ponds and streams are not only a pleasure to their owners, but in cities and towns they are often the only surviving habitats for beleaguered frogs, toads, newts, dragonflies and water plants.

PONDS AND MERES

Ponds, both natural and man-made, have always had a close relationship with human settlement. The words *mere* and *pool* nearly always relate to pre-historic or Anglo-Saxon naturally water-filled hollows whereas *pond*, a later, medieval term, perhaps originally meant those dug out for rearing fish. Throughout history these small areas of water have been used also as drinking holes for cattle, and in small industries such as metal-smelting and blacksmithing.

Conservationists estimate that in the last fifty years we have lost half of our ponds to urban development; those that survive are in rural villages, in woods or on protected heaths and commons. As the water disappears so do the dependent flora and fauna: gnarled and twisted willows, damsel flies, dragonflies, frogs, toads, newts and waterfowl. The endangered starfruit (*Damasonium alisma*) is now found in only three ponds in the south of England. It is a plant that was perfectly adapted to village ponds in which the water level rose and fell with the seasons and whose muddy margins were maintained by the trampling of cattle. Seeds were set into the mud and lay dormant until the low water levels in summer allowed the plant to put on foliage and grow.

Ponds need constant management if they are not to become silted up, choked with vegetation and eventually colonized by woodland trees. The major conservation organizations are doing much to restore and maintain our ponds, but local groups can often target and save those in their own area (see addresses p. 188).

BROADS

The Broads of Norfolk and north-east Suffolk are now recognized as the flooded remains of medieval peat workings and are not in any sense 'natural'. But over the last six hundred years or so they have developed a unique ecology and natural history that is as fascinating as that of any prehistoric mere. The Broads are a 150 mile complex of rivers and open water (broads), whose gentle flow and tree-fringed beauty has, in the last century, captivated thousands of leisure boaters in search of peace and quiet. Before this, the Broads were an important economic resource, supplying great quantities of fish, eels and waterfowl, and stout reeds for thatching. In the adjacent meadows, hay was grown and cut down in late summer before flooding in the winter. The typical Broads trees are willow and alder, which grow happily with their roots in water, and both were harvested for small poles and timber. The bankside vegetation is mainly bur-reed and flowering rush, some native water-lilies and water soldiers, bladderwort, frogbit, hornwort, and arrowhead.

But the Broads are changing at an alarming rate. Part of this change is inevitable, caused by the natural silting and encroachment of vegetation that would be expected in man-made lakes and rivers. But more harm is being done by the motorboat whose propellers leave a rushing wake that damages the banks and churns up the plants on the bottom. The delicate balance of the calcium-rich water is being unsettled by large influxes of phosphates, mainly from nearby arable fields, and tourists are adding to the pollution. Once the Broads were home to swallow-tail butterflies, hawker dragonflies, marsh harriers and fen orchids. Now all these species are rare. Conservationists are working hard to restore the balance, but in areas like this there will always be a conflict between farming, tourism, development and nature conservation.

A wetland habitat in The Lost Gardens of Heligan

PEAT BOGS

The north-western corner of Britain provides a wetland landscape in total contrast to the Norfolk Broads. Bogs are the most awesome of our natural habitats, eerie and

forbidding, but unique and precious none the less. The basis of a bog is sphagnum moss which, if it is allowed to grow and form layers over the centuries, eventually rots down to form peat. The moss acts like a giant sponge, holding rainwater and maintaining a delicate balance of nutrients and minerals. Raised bog can be thirty or more feet deep so that when you walk across it you are actually walking 10 m (30 ft) above the ground; blanket bogs have a thinner covering and are usually found on the steep, upland slopes of mountainous Scotland and Wales. Classic bogs can be found at Kilhern Moss in Dumfries, Claish Moss, Argyll, and Glasson Moss in Cumbria, but also in lowland areas like the Somerset Levels. It is the lowland bogs, like those in Somerset and on Thorne and Hatfield Moors near Doncaster, that are under the greatest pressure from development, particularly from peat extraction.

Conditions in a peat bog are not only permanently saturated but quite acidic as most of the nutrients are leached downwards and therefore not available to the plants. These conditions are ideal for the mosses (ten or more members of the Sphagnum genus are found in British peat bogs) and for plants like the bog myrtle (*Myrica gale*) and bog rosemary (*Andromeda polifolia*) which can live in low nutrient levels. Others have adopted more ingenious ways of getting food. Carnivorous plants, like the sundew (*Drosera rotundiflora*), trap flies with their sticky tentacles while the butterworts (*Pinguicula* species) have sticky leaves with which to snare insects.

Peat bogs are under threat from all sides. Air pollution and acid rain may alter the delicate pH balance of +4 and kill the mosses, so in many ways bogs act like environmental barometers, warning us of changes in the atmosphere. Many have been drained to make them more useful for sheep grazing or game raising. Others have been planted with forestry trees; still others are being ploughed for peat – surely one of the most short-sighted forms of 'development'. Peat extraction scars the countryside, destroys thousands if not millions of years of archaeological and botanical records and supplies a product that can be easily replaced by more environmentally friendly alternatives. Conservation organizations have taken this seriously, and the peat campaign, spearheaded by ecologically minded gardeners, has proved that most garden plants grow quite well without it and that many of the uses for which peat is recommended, such as soil conditioning, would be better served by home-made garden compost and leaf moulds.

FRESHWATER MARSHES

Freshwater marshes are created wherever natural water, from a river, stream or lake, flows periodically into the surrounding grassland. Some marshes are permanently wet, others dry out considerably in the summer months. Marshes are found adjoining most of the major lowland rivers, around the Thames, the Stour in Suffolk, the Ouse in Cambridgeshire, the Nene in Northamptonshire and the Soar in Leicestershire. The plants that grow here include the marsh orchids, many species of sedge, and marsh cinquefoil. Water meadows are created when freshwater flows into surrounding grassland (see p.51).

FENLAND

Fen occurs in many parts of Britain, but the area most associated with this habitat is the fens around the Wash in Cambridgeshire, Lincolnshire and parts of Norfolk. Like the upland peat bogs or the Broads, the fens have a distinctive topography and natural history. The East Anglian fens include areas of salt-marsh near the coast, freshwater silt marsh a little way inland and freshwater peat marsh further inland still. This suggests a very wet landscape, but the fens we see today are disappointingly dry. Drained first by the Romans and by successive settlers throughout the Middle Ages, the largest-scale draining took place in the seventeenth century under the direction of Dutch engineers.

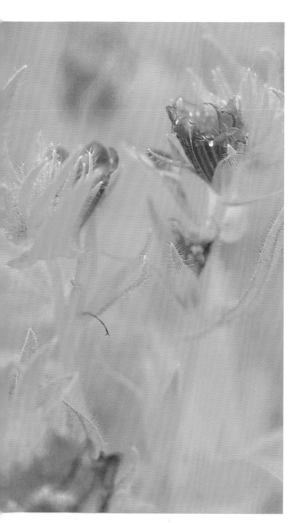

Today the fens are an agricultural landscape of large fields and few trees, and the original 'fen' survives in only a few pockets, such as Wicken Fen. Here, visitors can get a glimpse of what the fen landscape might have looked like a thousand years ago: tussocks of sedge, willows and water provide a habitat for around two hundred species of bird, including the bittern and heron. Greater spearwort, water dropwort, lesser water plantain and water-lilies survive in the water and hemp agrimony, water forget-me-not and purple loosestrife thrive on the damp margins. It is also home to disappearing plants such as the fen violet (*Viola persicifolia*) and the fen orchid (*Liparis loeselii*). Fens, like all the other wetland environments, were 'worked' and used by local people. Buckthorn and willow were coppiced for fuel and fencing, fen sedge was used for thatching, and reed grass was harvested for cattle bedding. The waterways were fished for eels and used to trap wildfowl.

Rough marsh mallow (Althaea hirsuta) is native to Southern Europe and Western Asia

Many plants thrived because of these activities – the fen orchid, for example, flowers best in the one or two years after reeds have been cut – and if a fen is no longer managed, many species die out. These carefully maintained fragments of fenland are a good place to see water plants growing in their natural environment and to get ideas for using water in the garden.

THE GARDEN WETLAND

Gardens on damp, boggy sites are often described as 'difficult' or 'problem' gardens. However, a naturally wet area is a real opportunity for a gardener to create their own mini-wetland and to plant moisture-loving species. Far from being a second-rate garden, these areas allow you to grow a host of native and exotic plants like bog primulas and astilbes that would not thrive in drier conditions. Not everyone has a naturally damp garden but it is relatively easy to create a pond or bog garden to increase the range of plants and to encourage wildlife. Plants such as water-lilies, flag irises and arrowhead like to have their roots submerged, but many more are happy in damp soil, and this includes the typical marshland plants such as marsh marigold, hemp agrimony, bogbean, monkey flower and ragged robin. Whether the garden is a natural wetland or a created one, the range of plants is among the most attractive and satisfying to grow.

Myriophyllum aquaticum *and bog bean grows in the shallow water, while purple loosestrife clings to the boggy margins*

INTRODUCING WATER
INTO THE GARDEN

The idea of making a pond is immediately attractive, but it is worth giving some thought to the style and siting before going ahead. Ill-conceived ponds may look unnatural and, although they will undoubtedly attract wildlife, they may also appear isolated unless they are incorporated into a wild area. Siting is the most crucial decision. Natural-looking ponds need to be quite large with gently sloping edges, so there should be enough space to allow for a pond about 4–5 m (12–15 ft) across. It should be away from overhanging trees that will cast too much shade and shed leaves that will eventually choke it. A pond and young children do not go together and unless you can securely fence off the area, it would be best to wait until the children are older before making one. If the garden already has a natural hollow that tends to get damp, then make use of it. A pond works best when it is not sited in the middle of a dry 'desert' of mown grass or shingle, but when at least one of the sides can have taller vegetation, such as meadow grass or shrubs,

Flowing water creates the ideal conditions for the monkey flower (Mimulus), *bottom right of picture*

and ideally an adjoining well-planted marshy area. This means that pond wildlife, particularly frogs and toads, will have an accessible area of cover when they need to crawl out of the water. It also makes it safer for birds to use the water for drinking and washing as they can retreat to the vegetation when cats or other predators approach.

MAKING A POND

The best way to make a pond is to use a flexible liner that can be bought in a sheet of the right size. Butyl liners are the most hard-wearing and the most expensive, but cheaper plastic ones will do the job.

◆ Choose a level piece of ground and mark out the pond area, using a hosepipe or short canes and string. A simple oval shape is best, but allow for a large shallow area on one or more sides for the marginal plants.

◆ Strip off the turf and dig out the pond. It is important to have a deep section in the centre and remember to allow for the thickness of the liner.

◆ As a rough guide, dig the hole to 90 cm (3 ft) at its deepest part, making the sides slope gently to ground level. It is essential to keep checking the level of the sides to make sure that one is not higher than the other. This can be done using a straight length of timber across the pond and a spirit level.

◆ Remove any sharp stones and cover the bottom of the pond with a layer of sand or carpet underlay to provide a cushion for the liner.

◆ Lay in the liner, aiming to eliminate any rucks or folds. Anchor the edges with bricks or stones. A small pile of stones in the centre will make sure the liner is secure. Make sure the liner overlaps the edge by at least 30 cm (12 in).

◆ Fill the pond with water using a hosepipe, easing off the edging stones as necessary. If you can collect enough rainwater in butts around the garden, fill the pond with this – it will contain fewer chemicals and the pond will have a better chance of establishing a healthy ecological balance. Cut off any extra liner and cover the edges with turf or paving stones.

◆ Add garden soil, the poorer quality the better – riddled to get rid of large stones – to the pond. Sand and gravel mix could be used as an alternative. This will settle and give the plants something to root into. Leave the pond for a week or two for the water to clear before planting.

PLANTING THE POND

A pond needs three types of plant to establish a successful ecosystem. Oxygenating plants, like hornwort or spiked water milfoil, are the first to go in, usually bought in weighted bunches which can be thrown into the pond where they will sink to the bottom. They will come with their own microscopic creatures and will soon aerate the water and help to keep it clear.

Nymphaea 'James Brydon' needs a water depth of 1m (3ft)

Then put in some aquatic plants, those that root on the bottom but produce their leaves on the surface, like water-lilies and frogbit. The leaves provide some shade on the water surface, which in turn prevent sunlight from creating too much algae. When introducing floating-leaved plants like water-lilies, it is a good idea to leave them in their baskets at first, placed on a pile of bricks in the centre of the pond, high enough to ensure that the leaves will float on the surface. As the stem grows, you can gradually lower the basket until the roots can be planted on the bottom of the pond without submerging the leaves.

In the shallow water at the edge of the pond, plant the marginals, like bogbean, marsh marigold and flag iris, which will link the pond to the rest of the garden. Only their roots are in water – and at some times of the year just in damp soil – while their stems, leaves and flowers tower upwards.

POND WEEDS AND OXYGENATORS

Hornwort (*Ceratophyllum demersum*)

Spiked Water Milfoil (*Myriophyllum spicatum*)

Curled Pondweed (*Potamogeton crispus*)

Water Crowfoot (*Ranunculus peltatus*)

Water Starwort (*Callitriche stagnalis*)

Water Violet (*Hottonia palustris*)

MAKING A BOG GARDEN

If you already have a boggy area in your garden, then developing a bog garden might simply be a case of watching what grows naturally and selectively weeding out plants that are either too rampant or too coarse. However, many people want to create a bog or marsh from scratch as a habitat for moisture-loving plants. If you have young children, a bog garden might be a safer alternative to a pond, however shallow. Success will depend on whether or not the area can be kept constantly moist. It should never dry out completely even in summer. If you live in a high-rainfall area this should not be a problem, but in dry areas you may need to top it up during drought periods.

◆ Choose a site away from overhanging trees that are likely to shed their leaves on to the area. However, a bog garden can be in a partially shaded part of the garden and most of the plants will flourish.

◆ Lay out the shape of the area. Like the pond, a simple oval is best or a lagoon or crescent shape if the boggy area is to curve round another feature. Make the area as large as your garden will allow. Many marsh plants are naturally spreading and look best if they can be given free rein. If the large area makes access difficult to other parts of the garden, consider making or buying a walkway of wooden decking to connect the dry areas.

◆ Remove the turf and top soil and make a gentle bowl or hollow to a depth of 45–60 cm (18–24 in). Lay a plastic or pvc liner in the hole, leaving a 30 cm (12 in) overlap all around. Make some holes in the base of the liner.

◆ Add a layer of gravel over the liner to improve drainage. Bog gardens need to be moist, but water also needs to be able to percolate down through the soil, through the base of the liner and back into the ground, otherwise it will become stagnant.

◆ Fill the hollow with a moisture-retentive soil. The excavated soil should be suitable. If it is too light or sandy, mix it with potting compost, leaf mould or garden compost. Take the soil over the edge of the hollow to disguise the liner. The plants will soon grow out and cover the edges, making it blend in naturally with the rest of the garden.

◆ Soak the bog garden thoroughly with a hosepipe before planting.

◆ Planting can begin straight away, using container-grown plants. Remember that many marsh and bog plants will spread to 60 cm (2 ft) or more, so leave plenty of room for them to grow. Check the average spread for each plant and arrange them accordingly.

BOG GARDEN MAINTENANCE

Check the moisture of the soil regularly and, if necessary, run a hosepipe to the area and set the water flow to trickle in gradually. In autumn, cut back dying foliage so that it does not choke the garden. When it starts to become overgrown, lift and divide plants in autumn or spring.

In naturally moist, shady areas, a dense planting of foliage suppresses weeds and cuts down maintenance

WETLAND PLANTS

When we look at the way water plants behave in the wild, we are given clues to how they will behave in the garden. Plants that grow naturally by streams or at the edge of a pond need similar conditions in the garden – it seems an obvious point but too many people struggle to grow wetland plants in dry soils and vice versa. One of the important features of wetland plants is that they propagate themselves through the water: in nature, either the seed is carried downstream or the water breaks off pieces of root, which then become lodged elsewhere along the stream- or river-bank. In a garden setting, where the water is more likely to be still than running, it is more usual to increase plants by division, lifting and replanting the clumps in the autumn or spring. However, if there is moving water in the garden, plants may seed and root themselves naturally.

The principles of wild gardening outlined for the other habitats in this book apply equally to the wetland parts of the garden. The aim should be to keep the planting as natural as possible, to choose plants that will be happy in the existing conditions and to plant them closely together so that they act as natural weed suppressants. There is no question of using weedkillers, pesticides or fertilizers in a wild water garden: water plants are particularly sensitive to chemicals and adding even small amounts would destroy the delicate balance of plant and animal life. Plants should be allowed to self-seed and root wherever they choose; if they become overgrown they can easily be pulled out by hand. In fact, the main maintenance job for a wetland garden is to lift and split overgrown plants and to replant them elsewhere. Even if the pond or bog garden is in a restricted space, it is still worth including some of the more vigorous species and weeding them out when they threaten to take over. Selective weeding is one of the most efficient ways to keep a wetland within bounds, and although some gardeners are loath to pull out plants they have spent months nurturing, it is important to do it to maintain a good mix of species.

MARSH AND BOG PLANTS

It is easy to be dismissive of non-native plants, but for wild gardeners there is nothing to be gained from being too purist. Most astilbes emanate from China, Japan, Pakistan and the Himalayas, where they are found growing by the side of woodland streams and in ravines in the mountains. They all need a moist, preferably slightly acid soil and are perfect for a bog garden or pond-side planting, where they will form substantial clumps of ferny leaves and produce tall plumes of white, cream, pink or red flowers.

The monkey flower is a good example of a plant that is both native and exotic. There are two naturalized monkey flowers in Britain, the heavily spotted *Mimulus guttatus*, which is local to Scotland, Wales and a few areas in northern England, and the bright yellow *M. luteus*, which is more widespread. They have escaped into the countryside and made themselves completely at home, rooted in the bank of a river or stream with the flowers and leaves out in the clear, flowing water. Only the gaudy colouring suggests they have not always been part of the landscape. In fact, the spotted mimulus is a native of Chile and the yellow form is from the western states of the USA.

Yet they have adapted perfectly to wild places and to gardens, where they will grow in any moist soil by water.

One of the earliest wetland plants to flower is the marsh marigold or kingcup (*Caltha palustris*). In the wild it is found growing in damp ditches, at streamsides, in wet woodland, in marshes and fens, and it is native to many countries of the northern hemisphere. In the garden it can be grown in the damp soil and shallow water at the edge of a pond or in a bog garden. It does not have any specific soil requirements – except that the ground must not dry out completely – and will form substantial clumps in the right conditions. The shining yellow flowers appear at the beginning of spring and may continue intermittently until the end of summer. There are some double-flowered garden forms, which look rather fussy, but the single white variety *alba* has more of the spirit of the original.

Most of the primula family prefer a moist soil (the exception is the cowslip, see p.63). Oxlips and wild primroses are often found growing by streams in the countryside, but in the garden we can extend the range by planting some of the many Asiatic primroses that also enjoy these cool, moist conditions. Much is written in gardening books about how to make primroses 'survive', when if only we would plant them nearer to their natural habitat – water – they would not need any encouragement. The Asiatic primroses are exciting for the wild gardener, making larger clumps than the natives and having tall upright flowers. One of the largest is *Primula pulverulenta*, a native of west Sichuan where it grows in wet places by streams. It produces stunning flowers 1 m (3 ft) high on stems that carry the deep rose-pink candelabra blooms all the way down, in June and July. It prefers an acidic, peaty soil. Somewhat shorter, but otherwise quite similar in appearance, is *P. beesiana*, which is better for neutral or slightly alkaline soils. It flowers later, from July to August. If the edge of a pond or bog garden is in

Astilbe 'Vesuvius' and pulmonarias thrive in a shady bog garden

shade, the giant cowslip (*P. florindae*) would be a good choice. It has tall stems with a small pale yellow umbel of flowers at the top, which give off a spicy scent. Grown singly the flowers can look dejected but in a group of five or more they are magnificent. The plant needs room to spread, though: its foliage can reach almost 1 m (3 ft) across. If you don't have room for anything so large, the Himalayan cowslip (*P. sikkimensis*) is less forceful and makes a pretty carpet of early summer flowers.

Many of the native British wetland plants could also find a place on the damp soil of a wild garden. Ragged robin (*Lychnis flos-cuculi*) is one of the prettiest with its pink, fringed summer flowers, which are very attractive to bees and butterflies. This could be grown alongside the scented, frothy cream flowers of meadowsweet (*Filipendula ulmaria*) and the smaller marsh valerian (*Valeriana dioica*) with its clusters of pale pink flowers. The tall-growing perennial yellow loosestrife (*Lysimachia vulgaris*) makes a good show, particularly where it is shady, and the marsh could be edged with its low-growing relative *L. nummularia*, creeping Jenny. There is also a tall purple loosestrife

Monkey Flower
(*Mimulus guttatus*)

(*Lythrum salicaria*), which on neutral or alkaline soils will flourish and flower from June to August. Like the yellow loosestrife, it is attractive to bees and butterflies. If you have an area where you can accommodate a big, bold plant try hemp agrimony (*Eupatorium cannabinum*), which grows up to 2 m (6 ft) tall and will attract a mass of butterflies to its flat pink flower-heads. The kindest description of its looks was by Geoffrey Grigson in *The Englishman's Flora*; he says its colour is 'raspberry and cream', whereas in reality it is quite a dull pink. One plant that should be considered for moist ground is the Grass of Parnassus (*Parnassia palustris*), a white plant similar to the marsh marigold, which has seriously declined in the wild due to the draining of many lowland marshes. It was named, confusingly, after the holy mountain of the god Apollo, but it is neither a mountain plant nor a grass.

WATER PLANTS

For many people, ponds and pools are for growing water-lilies, fascinating plants that adapt to changing water levels by elongating their stems according to seasonal conditions,

so that their roots are always on the bottom and their leaves always on the surface. However, our native water-lily (*Nymphaea alba*) is too large for most suburban gardens and even with its natural adaptability needs a planting depth of over 2 m (6 ft). The other native water-lilies are not popular because they don't look like conventional lilies: the

ABOVE LEFT: Purple Loosestrife (Lythrum salicaria)
ABOVE: Himalayan Balsam (Impatiens glandulifera)

yellow water-lily (*Nuphar lutea*), for example, looks more like a marigold or kingcup with small globular flower-heads that rise out of the water rather than lying on the surface. The fringed water-lily (*Nymphoides peltata*) is, in fact, a member of the bogbean family; its small yellow flowers are not particularly lily-like and in small ponds it would be

difficult to control. For most people, then, the choice is from one of the many garden hybrids that will be happy in a depth of about 1 m (3 ft) of water. *Nymphaea* 'Andreana' has cream-coloured flowers and spreads no more than 60 cm (2 ft) across. 'Moorei' has soft yellow blooms and only needs a planting depth of 45 cm (18 in). 'Mrs Richmond' is an old variety with classic pink flowers and again, will be happy in only 45–60 cm (18–24 in) of water. If the pond is small you could do without water-lilies altogether and plant one of the other floating natives instead, such as the frogbit (*Hydrocharis morsus-ranae*) with its bronze-green kidney-shaped leaves and white flowers, or the amphibious bistort (*Polygonum amphibium*) with its arrowhead leaves and deep pink flower spikes.

For the shallow water around the edge of the pond, water irises add stature and grandeur. Two species are found growing wild in Britain: the yellow flag iris (*Iris pseudacorus*), a true native seen on freshwater margins, and the purple flag iris (*Iris versicolor*), an incomer from North America that has made itself at home on the shores of Lake Ullswater in Cumbria, by the river Calder in Yorkshire and in parts of Perthshire. Both irises can be grown in a garden wetland, where they should be planted with their roots in soil, with 5–25 cm (2–10 in) of water above them. Both species are tall: the purple iris grows to 1 m (3 ft), the yellow iris to 2 m (6 ft) and both form substantial clumps that in the right conditions will spread to form a large colony. However, it is quite an easy matter to lift and divide the rhizomes after flowering to keep the clumps in check and to make new plants for other parts of the garden. A smaller species is the purple-flowered *Iris laevigata*, a native of Japan and Northern China, with a height of about 60 cm (2 ft). Iris rhizomes should be planted about 5 cm (2 in) beneath the soil in autumn or spring.

In larger ponds, with extensive areas of shallow water, some of the taller aquatics could be introduced. The sweet flag (*Acorus calamus*) makes a stout clump of leaves, which were traditionally cut and dried for strewing on the floors of houses – they have a sweet orangy smell when crushed. It looks rather like an iris or a reed, but it is actually a member of the arum family. This family, which includes the land-locked cuckoo pints, is represented in the water by the bog arum (*Calla palustris*), which looks rather like a small arum lily holding its leaves just above the water surface. The Americans have a similar, although much larger, species known as the skunk cabbage (*Lysichiton americanus*), which is widely grown in bog gardens and has a yellow spathe in contrast to the white spathe of the bog arum.

Water-lilies look best where there is room to allow them to spread and multiply freely

One of the most attractive rushes for the wild pond is the flowering rush (*Butomus umbellatus*). The leaves are narrow and more elegant than those of the irises and in late summer it produces a head of pink, cup-shaped flowers. Also distinctive is the arrowhead (*Sagittaria sagittifolia*), which has arrow-shaped leaves held above or just floating on the water and a tall stem of white flowers with a dark purple blotch on the base. The bogbean (*Menyanthes trifoliata*), although small in stature, has strong, creeping runners that can create a large clump with starry pink and white flowers in early summer.

SHRUBS FOR THE BOG GARDEN

Several shrubs can cope with waterlogged conditions and could be planted in a bog garden or around the edge of a pond – although not so close that the shade or their falling leaves would be a problem. The guelder rose (*Viburnum opulus*) is one of these, and in the wild it can be found growing in damp woodlands and fen. It is good for the smaller garden as it will stay below 4 m (12 ft) and has frothy white flowers in summer and bright red berries in autumn. Most of the elders (*Sambucus* species) also like damp soil. There is a particularly attractive golden-leafed form (*S. nigra* 'Aurea'), which has bright yellow leaves as long as it is planted in full sunshine, and a red elder (*S. racemosa*), which has red autumn berries instead of the usual black. Elders can be too fast-growing for small gardens but they can be easily coppiced every two or three years. Cutting them back makes the plant produce interesting stems and lots of young foliage in lieu of the flowers and berries.

Autumn foliage of the herbaceous bog garden plant, Darmera peltata, *a native of North California and South Oregon*

DEEP WATER PLANTS (AQUATICS)

	PLANTING DEPTH X SPREAD
Arrowhead (*Sagittaria sagittifolia*)	30–90 cm (1–3 ft) x 30 cm (1 ft)
Arrow-shaped leaves; white flowers with purple centre, July/August	
Fringed Water Lily (*Nymphoides peltata*)	60–90 cm (2–3 ft) x 90 cm (3 ft)
Round floating leaves; yellow fringed flowers, July to September	
Frogbit (*Hydrocharis morsus-ranae*)	30–90 cm (1–3 ft) x 30 cm (1 ft)
Floating kidney-shaped leaves, white flowers, July/August	
Water Soldier (*Stratiotes aloides*)	15–60 cm (6–24 in) x 30 cm (12 in)
Upright, pineapple-like leaves; white flowers, June to August	

NB The spreads given are for individual plants, but wetland plants can increase into substantial clumps, spreading wider than the measurements given.

SHALLOW WATER PLANTS (SEMI-AQUATICS)

HEIGHT X SPREAD

Amphibious bistort (*Polygonum amphibian*)　　　30 cm (1 ft) x 30–60 cm (1–2 ft)
　　Oblong floating leaves; pink upright flower spikes, June to August; creeping
　　perennial

Bog Arum (*Calla palustris*)　　　30 cm (1 ft) x 30–60 cm (1–2 ft)
　　Heart-shaped leaves; white spathe, June to August; red berries; rhizome.
　　Note: All parts of the plant are poisonous.

Bogbean (*Menyanthes trifoliata*)　　　30 cm (1 ft) x 60–90 cm (2–3 ft)
　　Oval leaves; starry pink and white flowers, April to June; creeping perennial

Iris laevigata　　　45–60 cm (18–24 in) x 30 cm (12 in)
　　Upright sword-shaped leaves; blue flowers, June/July; rhizome.
　　Note: All parts of the plant are poisonous.

Purple Flag Iris (*Iris versicolor*)　　　60 cm (2 ft) x 30 cm (1 ft)
　　Upright sword-shaped leaves; lilac-purple flowers, June to August; rhizome.
　　Note: All parts of the plant are poisonous.

Yellow Flag Iris (*Iris pseudacorus*)　　　60–90 cm (2–3 ft) x 30 cm (1 ft)
　　Upright, sword-shaped leaves; yellow flowers, June to August; rhizome.
　　Note: All parts of the plant are poisonous.

Sweet Flag (*Acorus calamus*)　　　60–90 cm (2–3 ft) x 30 cm (1 ft)
　　Upright, sword-shaped leaves (sweet-smelling when crushed); yellowish-green
　　flower cone, June/July; rhizome.

MARSH OR BOG PLANTS

HEIGHT X SPREAD

Astilbe chinensis var. *pumila*　　　30 cm (12 in) x 40 cm (16 in)
　　Compact rosettes of leaves; mauve-purple flower spikes, July to September;
　　perennial

Astilbe simplicifolia　　　23 cm (9 in) x 23 cm (9 in)
　　Dwarf plant with ferny leaves; pale pink flower spikes, July to September;
　　perennial

Astilbe 'Bressingham Beauty'　　　90 cm (3 ft) x 90 cm(3 ft)
　　Large, strong-growing plant; rose pink flowers, July/August; perennial

Creeping Jenny (*Lysimachia nummularia*)   2.5 cm (1 in) x 1 m (3 ft)
Carpeting plant with bright green leaves; shiny yellow flowers, June; creeping evergreen

Grass of Parnassus (*Parnassia palustris*)   30 cm (12 in) x 23 cm (9 in)
Heart-shaped leaves; white flowers with yellow stamens, June to September; perennial

Hemp Agrimony (*Eupatorium cannabinum*)   2 m (6 ft) x 1 m (3 ft)
Large clump-forming plant; divided leaves with serrated edges; dull pink flower-heads, July to September; perennial

Marsh Valerian (*Valeriana dioica*)   30–45 cm (12–18 in) x 30 cm (12 in)
Oval basal leaves; delicate pink flowers, May to July; perennial

Meadowsweet (*Filipendula ulmaria*)   1.5 m (5 ft) x 1 m (3 ft)
Dark green, lobed leaves; pale cream flat-headed flower clusters, June to September; perennial

Monkey flower (*Mimulus guttatus*)   45 cm (18 in) x 60 cm (24 in)
Oval, toothed leaves; yellow flowers spotted with dark red, July to September; perennial

Mimulus luteus   45 cm (18 in) x 60 cm (24 in)
Oval, toothed leaves; yellow flowers, July to September; perennial

Primula beesiana   30 cm (12 in) x 20 cm (8 in)
Large, mid-green leaves; candelabra-type deep rose flowers; May to July; perennial

Giant Cowslip (*Primula florindae*)   90 cm (34 in) x 30 cm (12 in)
Broad, basal leaves; large fragrant yellow flowers on upright stems, May to July; perennial

Primula pulverulenta   80 cm (32 in) x 23 cm (9 in)
Mid-green, toothed leaves; cerise flowers with dark eye, May to July; perennial

Himalayan Cowslip (*Primula sikkimensis*)   40 cm (16 in) x 23 cm (9 in)
Mid-green, basal leaves; yellow-cream pendent flowers, May to June; perennial

Purple Loosestrife (*Lythrum salicaria*)   1.2 m (4 ft) x 45 cm (18 in)
Upright plant; small, mid-green leaves; reddish-purple flower spikes, July; perennial

Ragged Robin (*Lychnis flos-cuculi*)   60 cm (2ft) x 40 cm (16in)
Pointed, deep-green leaves, delicate fringed pink flowers, June to September; spreading perennial

Skunk Cabbage (*Lysichiton americanus*)   1.2 m (4 ft) x 1.5 m (5 ft)
Huge leaves (30cm wide); 30 cm (1 ft) long yellow spathe, June to August; perennial

Yellow Loosestrife (*Lysimachia vulgaris*)   1 m (3 ft) x 90 cm (3 ft)
Spreading plant; long, elliptical leaves; loose yellow flower spikes, July; perennial

WETLAND WILDLIFE

A garden wetland may not be able to support or emulate even a fraction of the thousand of species found in the wild, but just introducing a pond, or planting marsh plants, will greatly increase the amount of wildlife in the garden. In urban areas, garden ponds are often the only areas in which frogs, toads and newts can live and breed. They will spend the spring and summer in and around the pond, but come autumn they will emerge to hibernate in a damp compost heap, the base of a drainpipe, in a log pile or under a stone; frogs will also bury themselves in the mud at the edge of the pond until the spring. Newts are happy in quite small areas of water so are ideal for garden ponds. The smooth newt is the one most commonly found in garden ponds and is shyer and less noisy than frogs or toads, spending most of its life underwater. The tadpoles are easy to recognize as they look like miniature versions of the adults, complete with legs. It is not a good idea to

move adult amphibians from their home – they will travel to other ponds naturally, and if there is a watery habitat in your neighbourhood you may find they just turn up in your garden, but if you want to introduce them it is better to move them at the tadpole stage. If in doubt, contact your local wildlife trust (see p. 188). The best way to introduce all the smaller creatures to a new pond is to import a bucketful of mud and sludge from the bottom of an established pond. This will ensure that the new pond has lots of larvae and eggs to start a new generation of water insects.

The most conspicuous insects associated with wetlands are the damsel flies and dragonflies. There are around forty different species in Britain and their dazzling colours and lacy wings make them attractive garden visitors. The dragonfly is bolder and more powerful in flight, making darting movements rather than the more gentle fluttering of the smaller damsel fly. In spring, they will lay their eggs just under the water on the leaves of reeds and irises. The egg hatches into a larva or 'nymph', which may spend several years

Riverbanks, reedbeds and estuaries are the natural haunt of the otter

underwater before crawling up the stem to emerge into the air as a fully fledged dragonfly. Once grown they feed on insects, snatched from the air in mid-flight. Water beetles dive and skate over the surface of the pond in search of small bugs, and pond skaters feed on hapless insects that have fallen into the water.

Few butterflies are associated specifically with ponds and water, but any increase in plant populations will lead to an increase in butterflies. Moisture-loving plants like lady's smock (*Cardamine pretensis*) provide food for caterpillars of the orange-tip butterfly, and elephant hawk moths feed on the bogbean (*Menyanthes trifoliata*). Purple loosestrife (*Lythrum salicaria*) is popular with large white butterflies, while ragged robin (*Lychnis flos-cuculi*) and hemp agrimony (*Eupatorium cannabinum*) provide summer nectar for all species. The rare swallowtail butterfly found in the East Anglian fens has specific caterpillar food plants, which include the moisture-loving milk parsley (*Peucedanum palustre*). The marsh fritillary butterfly, found mainly in the west of Britain, also has a liking for damp boggy places and uses water plantains and devilsbit scabious (*Succisa pratensis*) as its food plants.

The shallow waters at the edge of a pond will make a good watering and washing place for blackbirds, sparrows, thrushes and most other garden birds. Pied wagtails will

Purple loosestrife is an easy to grow plant for the damp soil at the edge of the pond

approach to drink and peck small insects from the mud. Swallows and swifts will swoop low over ponds and bog gardens to collect insects. Shallow-edged ponds are also good, as a water supply for nocturnal mammals, like hedgehogs, foxes and badgers if they are in the neighbourhood.

WHERE TO SEE...
WETLANDS AND WETLAND PLANTS

Local ponds, streams and rivers should be the first port of call for those in search of wetlands. In urban areas, flooded gravel pits and other reclaimed industrial sites have often been turned into wetland habitats. Contact the local wildlife trust or urban conservation organization for details of local reserves. The Norfolk Broads and the Lake District are well publicized and well documented, and they are certainly still worth visiting.

Saltwells Nature Reserve
Pedmore Road, Brierley Hill, Dudley, West Midlands, telephone 01384 812795. *The largest wholly urban reserve in Britain. In early summer sheets of orchids can be seen, and later a wide variety of wetland plants.*

The Wildfowl and Wetlands Trust
Slimbridge, Gloucestershire GL2 7BT, telephone 01453 890333. *Set up for the conservation of wildfowl and their supporting habitats, the trust manages a network of wetland reserves and visitors' centres in the UK.*

Wicken Fen National Nature Reserve
Lode Lane, Wicken, Ely, Cambridgeshire CB7 5XP, telephone 01353 720274. *A unique fragment of the fenland habitat that once covered large tracts of East Anglia. Owned and managed by the National Trust.*

Wetland Garden
Fast Rabbit Farm, Ash Cross, Nr. Dartmouth, Devon, telephone 01803 712437. *Garden open under the National Gardens Scheme. Specialist nursery open daily, but check opening times before visiting.*

The Henry Doubleday Research Association
Ryton Organic Gardens, Coventry CV8 3LG, telephone 01203 303517. E-mail : enquiry@hdra.demon *Supplies information about reed bed construction and all aspects of organic gardening.*

Chapter 4

Seas

hore

COASTAL HABITATS ARE AMONG the most beautiful places in Britain but they are also the most inhospitable for wild plants. Exposed to strong, salty winds and strong sunlight, suffering drought and occasional drenching by brackish seawater, anchored in poor soil on free-draining sand or shingle, the seashore plants live in a far from ideal environment. Yet, as with all natural habitats, some plants have not only adapted to these

harsh conditions but positively flourish in them. Most of our major plant families, including campions, daisies, thrifts and brassicas, have one or more species represented on the seashore. In this chapter, we shall take seashore to mean cliffs and ledges, shingle beaches, sand dunes, salt marshes and beaches which, as with other natural habitats, may have important parallels with situations in our own gardens.

Many gardens have echoes of the seashore environment even if they are nowhere near the coast. An exposed garden on a hillside or in a high-rise development bears a more than passing resemblance to a natural cliff top. Both have to contend with strong, drying winds and lack of shade. Similarly, gardeners with dry, poor soils will recognize the problems that growing plants on sand poses, particularly in areas where summer droughts are becoming a regular occurrence. By looking at how wild plants cope with these conditions we will be better prepared to choose plants that thrive and look good in our own gardens. Many of the wild plants themselves can be grown as garden plants and will thrive no matter how poor the soil, or how dry and exposed the site.

SALT MARSHES

Salt marshes are formed where streams and rivers meet the sea. Silts from the inland river are deposited in the estuary and the result is a landscape of mud-flats and meandering creeks. Each day freshwater meets seawater and the mud is washed by a tidal influx of salty water. It is the perfect environment for wading birds like the curlew, oystercatcher and redshank, and for geese and shelducks. It is also home to plants like marsh samphire or glasswort, sea lavender, sea asters and sea plantain which have adapted their own particular mechanisms for dealing with these unique conditions. Salt marshes can be found all around the coasts of Britain from the Solway Firth to Carmarthen Bay. They cover huge areas of land: 17,000 hectares (42,000 acres)

Rock Samphire (Crithmum maritimum) - local to the coasts of Suffolk and the south-west

at Morecambe Bay, for example, and 23,700 hectares (58,562 acres) at the Wash. Not surprisingly, then, these areas are always under pressure from groups who want to 'improve' them – that is, to seal them off from the sea, drain and reclaim them for agriculture. They are also constantly under threat from development as industrial sites and extended port facilities, so it has become vitally important to recognize and protect the seashore's unique flora.

Low down on the shoreline the first plants to colonize these shallow waters are the glassworts, the best known of which is the edible marsh samphire (*Salicornia europea*), harvested on many coasts and sold in local markets and restaurants. It is picked in late summer and eaten rather like asparagus, with butter, although it is saltier. Local folklore has it that samphire must be washed by the tide to be any good, and this is more than just an old wives' tale. The shiny, succulent stems are designed to shrug off the mud and weeds of the tides easily so that when the water has retreated the surface of the plant is clean and ready to photosynthesize. Glassworts also have the ability to absorb any freshwater around them by osmosis.

Marsh Samphire (Salicornia europaea) *– a widespread plant, harvested for its edible young stems*

At the edge of the salt marsh the boundary with the beach or dunes is often marked by seablites (*Sueda vera*), which form a shrubby zone along the drift line. Seablites are extremely resistant plants, able to adapt to changing levels of sand and shingle and building up into substantial shrubs over 1 m (3 ft) high. On the banks of the salty creeks there will be sea purslane (*Halimione portulacoides*), a spreading shrub with silvery-grey leaves and yellow flower panicles in summer. Seablites and sea purslane are tough, binding plants that anchor themselves in the mud so as not to get washed away by the tides. As the marsh gets drier there will be sea lavender (*Limonium vulgare*), a low-growing plant with pinkish purple flowers. It is not as striking as true lavender, but when it occurs in great swaths as it sometimes does on the north Norfolk coast in late summer, it conjures up images of the perfumed lavender fields of Provence. On the Channel Islands a rare form, known as Alderney sea lavender, occurs and can be found clinging to rocks in the seas around the coasts. Another pretty plant is the sea aster (*Aster tripolium*), which edges the banks of salty creeks with bright purple daisy-like flowers in late summer. This is a relative of the garden asters with the same central yellow disc and rays of petals, but its fleshy stem and leaves help it withstand the saline conditions.

DUNES AND BEACHES

Sandy beaches, dunes and even shingle are Britain's favourite summer-holiday destinations. Many people recognize and respect the seashore environment, but many more treat it like a giant playground, trampling plants and grasses and leaving litter behind them. The seashore is at risk not only from individuals, but also from large-scale oil and chemical pollution, and from sewage. While we may not be able to do much about the major problems, we can learn how this fragile ecosystem of plants works and perhaps be more persuasive in lobbying for its survival.

This is the home of sea kale, sea heath, the yellow horned poppy, sea hollies and marram grass, all perfectly adapted to a diet of pure sand and salt air. Marram grass has tube-like leaves that minimize evaporation and make it resistant to drought. The sea hollies have thorny, waxy leaves that deter predators and conserve moisture. The yellow horned poppy (*Glaucium flavum*) has a deep tap-root that travels 2 m (6 ft) or more in search of freshwater and the sea heath forms branching mats that stabilize the sand and shingle, and tiny, rolled-up leaves that resist wind and drought. Sea kale (*Crambe maritima*) often accumulates where there is a concentration of deposited seaweed on the shoreline, which provides it with nutrients. It has another adaptive device, a waxy coating to the leaves, which helps to reduce water loss.

Marram grass on Studland Beach, Dorset

Just above the tide line there may be sea plantain (*Plantago maritimus*) or buck's-horn plantain (*P. coronopus*), both fairly unremarkable plants with narrow grass-like leaves and yellowish-brown flower spikes. Yet plantains are important exactly because they are so ubiquitous and resilient to difficult habitats (other members of the family grow on dry grasslands, on wastelands and on poor soils). On the upper part of the beach, there may be tough pink-flowering sea rocket (*Cakile maritima*), an annual colonizer of young sand dunes, which tolerates salt spray and helps to stabilize the sand, or the creeping sea sandwort (*Honkenya peploides*), which does the same job. One of the prettiest dune or shingle plants is the sea heath (*Frankenia laevis*), which has purplish flowers in late summer that bear a resemblance to heather, although it is not from the same family. The sea heath's leaves are rolled under at the margins to conserve moisture and it forms a dense mat, helping to stabilize the shifting sand. In a seemingly barren landscape, grasshoppers and sandflies dart between these plants and a surprising number of bees and butterflies make the long flights along the shoreline vegetation.

COASTAL CLIFFS

Just above the beach in many parts of Britain, the limestone or granite drops away steeply to form cliffs and ledges that have their own plant communities. The most famous limestone cliffs are on the south coast, at Beachy Head in Sussex and Portland Bill in Dorset, and for granite cliffs the best locations are in Devon and Cornwall. The

main problems that plants have to contend with in these places is the lack of freshwater
and the salt winds, but they have adapted to this in a number of ways. On the cliff top
there may be low-growing hummock plants, which can resist the
winds that whip across the cliffs. One of these plants is the sea thrift
(*Armeria maritima*), with its narrow leaves which have a reduced
surface area to combat water loss. This is a good plant for exposed
gardens because it can withstand wind, drought and exposure to full sunlight. On grassy
cliff tops there may be bird's foot trefoil (*Lotus corniculatus*) and sea clover (*Trifolium
squamosum*), although the latter is now quite rare.

Dancing Ledge,
Isle of Purbeck, Dorset

On the cliff ledges and patches of shingle you may find the fleshy-leaved golden
samphire (*Inula crithmoides*), the white sea campion (*Silene uniflora*) or the Portland
spurge (*Euphorbia portlandica*), which have slightly succulent leaves that act as a water
reservoir, in the same way as those of a cactus. Other plants have long roots, which
anchor them to rock crevices and go deep into the cracks and fissures to draw out water,
such as the sea beet (*Beta vulgaris*) and the wild cabbage (*Brassica oleracea*). These
plants provided the original stock for the cultivated beets and cabbages we now grow in
the vegetable garden. Seashore plants must propagate mainly by wind-blown seed, and
the Danish scurvy-grass (*Cochlearia danica*) is one of the small, low-growing annuals
that flower on the cliff tops from February onwards. Its seeds can scatter over a large
distance and it has often been found growing on disturbed ground, such as roadsides, in
inland locations.

SEASHORE GARDENS

Some of us try to garden in plots near to the coast and are already familiar with the
seashore environment, but many more struggle with gardens that have a whole series of
'seashore' problems. Houses on newly built estates often have gardens where there are
no trees for shade and the soil is impoverished and dry, equally tower-block balconies
have to contend with fierce drying winds. Many people in the south and east of Britain
are having to deal with hotter summers, longer periods of drought and water restrictions
and their gardens are turning into deserts. The idea of a 'dry, seaside garden' where the
plants would enjoy these conditions is more appealing than a constant struggle against
the elements.

One of the principles of wild gardening is to go with the forces of nature, not to
battle against them. Therefore, if the garden is hot, dry and windy, we need to seek out
plants that are adapted to these conditions. If we insist on trying to grow plants that
would be more at home on the woodland floor, when these cool, shady conditions just do
not exist, we are doomed to failure. As always, it could make good ecological sense to see
your garden, or part of it, as a mini-seashore and to enhance the naturally dry, sun-baked
conditions rather than try to alter them.

GARDENING ON SANDY SOIL

You will probably know already if your soil is sandy – it will be light and easy to dig and it will dry out very quickly. When you pick it up it will crumble quickly through your fingers, and in hot, dry spells it turns to dust or sand. The main problem with this kind of soil is that it lacks nutrients and structure; there is no humus and any feeding from the top is quickly leached away. But it also has some important benefits: it warms up quickly in spring and summer, and it does not get waterlogged; it is much kinder to plants in cold, wet spells and, in fact, sandy soils can often support tender plants through the winter far better than heavy soils. It is possible to improve sandy soils by digging in humus-rich materials, such as old mushroom compost, garden compost, leaf mould or well-rotted manure, and this will help the soil structure to retain more moisture and nutrients. A mulch of the same materials or of bark will also help to cut down water loss. However, the best way to deal with sandy soils is to choose plants that enjoy this warm, free-draining environment. Try to forget the usual rules of gardening, which are that we must all strive to create a 'normal' soil, and instead create a garden that is in sympathy with the natural growing conditions. The alternative is a never-ending routine of watering and mulching, which is time-consuming and ultimately expensive.

USING TREES AND SHRUBS

One of the time-honoured ways of dealing with typical seaside gardens that are subject to high winds (and this can apply to lots of inland and urban gardens too) is to plant a protective belt of trees or shrubs to cut down the destructive and drying effects of the wind. This is effective and will help to stabilize the soil and protect the plants within the sheltered area. The trees need to be planted close together to form a good screen and could include poplar, birch, holly, oak and eucalyptus, all of which will grow on sandy soil. The evergreen holm oak (*Quercus ilex*) is a Mediterranean tree that enjoys a warm, well-drained soil, as do the white poplar (*Populus alba*) and many of the Mediterranean pines. However, not all gardens have room to accommodate a full-size tree shelter belt and in this case the best course of action would be to plant a

Sea Holly (Eryngium) *and grasses make an easy transition from the shoreline to the garden*

selection of hardy shrubs which in themselves can withstand the drying effects of the wind. Junipers, tamarisks, hebes, escallonias, elaeagnus and olearias will all thrive in this kind of environment. By taking clues from the way plants grow in exposed positions in the wild, it is possible to choose plants that will thrive with little or no protection at all.

COPING WITH WINDS

Apart from planting sheltering hedges and trees, there are other gardening techniques that can help to counteract the effect of fierce winds or gales, particularly in spring and autumn. If the garden is full of herbaceous plants, the temptation is to cut everything down in autumn as soon as it starts to look messy. Simply leaving the top growth of stems, foliage and seed-heads will offer some protection throughout the winter to the crowns of the plants underneath. The decaying plant matter will also help to act as a mulch, conserving moisture in the soil and adding some much-needed humus to light, sandy soils. Wind may also have a beneficial effect in that it allows the efficient dispersal of seed around the garden. One of the greatest joys of a wild garden is to see how plants reproduce and set seedlings in other areas – it is one of the signs by which we know that a plant is really at home. Many of the plants selected for seashore gardens are natural self-seeders and this will add to the uncontrived effect.

WILD COASTAL PLANTS

SALT MARSH PLANTS
Marsh Samphire (*Salicornia europaea*)
Shrubby Seablite (*Sueda vera*)
Sea Purslane (*Halimione portulacoides*)
Sea Lavender (*Limonium vulgare*)
Sea Aster (*Aster tripolium*)

BEACH AND DUNE PLANTS
Yellow Horned Poppy (*Glaucium flavum*)
Sea Kale (*Crambe maritima*)
Sea Rocket (*Cakile maritima*)
Sea Sandwort (*Honkenya peploides*)
Sea Heath (*Frankenia laevis*)
Sea Plantain (*Plantago maritima*)
Buck's-horn Plantain (*Plantago coronopus*)

CLIFF TOP AND LEDGE PLANTS
Bird's Foot Trefoil (*Lotus corniculatus*)
Sea Clover (*Trifolium squamosum*)
Sea Thrift (*Armeria maritima*)
Golden Samphire (*Inula crithmoides*)
Sea Campion (*Silene uniflora*)
Portland Spurge (*Euphorbia portlandica*)
Sea Beet (*Beta vulgaris*)
Wild Cabbage (*Brassica oleracea*)
Danish Scurvy-grass (*Cochlearia danica*)

MAKING A 'SEASHORE' GARDEN

The most important point about a 'seashore' garden is that it does not have to be at the coast. Any garden, in town, country or village, that has to contend with drought, intense sunlight or exposure to winds will be suitable for this type of garden. The basic elements are an open site and a light soil – either sandy or shingle – which is low in nutrients. This style of garden could be part of a larger garden or a garden in itself: either way it gives the gardener a chance to create a low-maintenance scheme, using sand, shingle, wooden decking and lots of easy-care plants.

GROUNDWORK

The first step in preparing a seashore garden is ruthlessly to strip away what has already been growing on the site. Many of us struggle with lawns that are no more than brown, parched patches of turf and these will need to be removed. Similarly, if you have been trying to grow the wrong sort of plants – shade-loving primulas, for example, hostas, or any green, leafy foliage plants – the chances are that they will have become stunted and parched and should be removed to a shadier part of the garden.

◆ Dig over the area – if the soil is sandy this should not be difficult – and remove any weeds. If it is stony, it is best to remove the largest stones, although it will not matter if the basic soil is gritty. If you are trying to convert an area where the soil is heavy, then you will need to reduce the fertility and improve the drainage by adding builders' sand or grit, which can be bought by the bag from garden centres and builders' merchants.

◆ It is a good idea to draw the area on paper, marking out where you will want a seat, an eating area and paths. For the planting areas, avoid the shade of overhanging trees – in Mediterranean gardens, trees are traditionally used as the focus for sitting and eating areas, offering protection from the midday sun. Paths can be made of shingle, and wooden decking can be bought in ready-made panels and used to make terraces and areas for pots, chairs and tables.

◆ Mark out the areas that are to be covered with gravel or shingle. Rake over the ground to give a flat surface. Remember that you can plant through the stones so, if you want to, you can cover the whole area. However, if there is a large quantity of new plants to put in, it might be wise to plant first and put the shingle down around them afterwards.

◆ Spread the shingle evenly to a depth of about 8 cm (3 in). To avoid the problem of stones finding their way into the house on people's shoes, choose stones that are at least 2.5 cm (1 in) diameter.

◆ Overlay the shingle with decking, if required. The stones will prevent the wood from coming into contact with the earth and rotting.

PLANTING THE SEASHORE GARDEN

How the garden is planted is partly a matter of personal taste. Some people prefer to have the plants well spaced out (as they tend to be on the seashore) so that they look as if they have arrived naturally. Others like a more dense planting, with clearly defined borders and paths. The best time to plant is in early autumn or late spring, and it is a simple matter to clear away a patch of shingle, put in the new plant, water it thoroughly and re-cover the surface with the stones. The types of plants selected for the seashore garden will not need regular feeding, watering or mulching. The only maintenance will be a bit of selective weeding, although even this will hardly be necessary – the whole point is to see which plants seed naturally and want to make their home there.

Sun-loving lavender and gypsophila are essential components of the seashore garden

SEASHORE PLANTS

The plants that thrive in the seashore garden are those that can withstand drought, fierce sunlight and wind and can survive on a poor soil. These are conditions that we encounter not just at the seaside, but in many gardens, particularly ones where the owner has neither the time nor the inclination to spend time watering, feeding and nurturing their garden and where the plants have to stand quite a lot of neglect. The plants that do best tend to be (although not exclusively) those with silvery blue or grey leaves: somehow, this kind of dry, stony setting seems to suit them better than a background of lawn or dark green foliage plants. All the plants in this section need a minimum of watering and feeding.

SHRUBS FOR THE DRY GARDEN

Sea Buckthorn (Hippophae rhamnoides) *makes a good hedging shrub for a dry, exposed garden*

One of the best shrubs for a poor or sandy soil is the sea buckthorn (*Hippophäe rhamnoides*). This is a native of coastal cliffs and sand dunes, and although it occurs naturally, it is also planted deliberately on some beaches to bind the sand and stop it shifting. It has the capability to fix nitrogen from the air through bacteria in the root nodules, which means it is actually improving the soil as it grows. It is a very spiny shrub that gives good cover for nesting birds and makes an effective barrier from winds. It grows fast to about 4 m (12 ft) and, if planted in groups, makes effective hedging for an exposed site. The narrow silvery leaves do not lose moisture through transpiration so it can withstand long periods without water. It has no flowers to speak of, but masses of bright orange berries in late summer and early autumn, which are edible – although quite acidic – and said to be high in vitamin C.

Sea buckthorn belongs to the wider Elaeagnaceae family and several members of the *Elaeagnus* species are well known as tough, windbreak shrubs. The most widely grown are the cultivars of *E. pungens*, particularly 'Maculata', which has glossy green leaves with a gold band, and 'Frederici', which is marked with a paler cream colour. Both are easy-care evergreens that don't need pruning. Tree purslane (*Atriplex halimus*) is another shrub that resists the onslaught of salty winds and can be used as a screen in exposed gardens. It has the

Mediterranean tamarisk (Tamarix gallica) has naturalised on southern coasts, here at Durlston Head, Swanage

typical silver-grey leaves and is not as fast growing as the sea buckthorn, reaching about 2.4 m (8 ft) after five years. It belongs to the same family as the sea purslane, a much lower sub-shrub that grows wild along the salt marsh edge.

Tamarisks from Mediterranean Europe also work well in a dry garden. *Tamarix gallica* has become naturalized on the south and east coasts of England: it is a deciduous shrub, about 2 m (6 ft) tall, with purple bark, tiny grey-green leaves and pink summer flowers. A much larger species is *T. tetandra*, which will reach about 5 m (16 ft) high after ten years and has loose arching branches with light pink flowers in late spring and early summer. Another tough bush for a town or seaside garden is the daisy bush (*Olearia* x *haastii*). Olearias come from Australia and New Zealand and are sun-loving and resistant to pollution, salt spray and winds. *O.* x *haastii* makes a compact, rounded hedge or single bush, 1–2 m (3–6 ft) high, and has masses of fragrant daisy-like white flowers in midsummer.

Escallonias have earned their reputation as coastal plants in the gardens of the milder west coasts of Britain, where gardeners have valued them for their ability to withstand salt-laden winds and sea mists. They are natives of South America and, although they are tough, they cannot stand extreme winter cold and are not always hardy. One of the best – and hardiest – of the garden cultivars is *Escallonia* 'Apple Blossom', a compact evergreen shrub with two-tone pink and white flowers in early summer which often appear intermittently until the autumn. This variety will grow no higher than 1.5 m (5 ft) and can be used for hedging. Cultivars of *E. rubra* are also hardy and the variety *macrantha* is a strong grower with deep crimson blossom. Escallonias don't need pruning and as long as the soil is well drained should survive for many years.

A shrub found growing wild on sand dunes, and which works well in a 'seashore' garden, is the burnet rose (*Rosa pimpinellifolia*). It is easily distinguishable from other wild roses by the autumn hips, which are purplish-black rather than the usual red, and by the leaves, which are more like those of salad burnet than a typical rose, hence its name. It forms a dense, very prickly shrub, with upright stems and single white flowers from May to July. It grows naturally on poor soils and without water, so will survive in a dry garden without any fussing.

TREE MALLOWS

The tree mallow (*Lavatera arborea*) found growing around the western coasts of Britain, particularly on cliffs, is not actually a tree or even a shrub, but a tall, woody-stemmed biennial, which can reach 3 m (9 ft) or more in a single season. This is one instance where breeding has really improved on the wild version and the garden lavateras have a better shrub-like shape, but with the same pretty pink flowers. Plants like *Lavatera* 'Candy Floss' and 'Barnsley' are fast-growing shrubs and therefore excellent for new gardens, where they will give an established air very quickly. The flowers on the cultivated versions are larger than the wild species and appear freely from July until the first frosts. Lavateras take up a lot of space, easily spreading 2 m (6 ft) across and up to 3 m (9 ft) high, but they can be pruned hard every spring to keep them under control. There is the more compact *Lavatera maritima* from the Mediterranean, which reaches only 1 m (3 ft) high and has small pink-flushed flowers. All lavateras love free-draining soil and sunshine so make ideal plants for a shingle or Mediterranean-style garden. Lavateras are at their best in their first few years: after this time, the flowers become less prolific and the trunk starts to get too woody. Old plants tend to grow top heavy and to fall over and split; it is best to pull them up and replace them.

LAVENDER

Few people have the true seaside conditions for sea lavender, but dry gardens on light soil are ideal for true lavender (*Lavandula* species). In fact, there is only one thing guaranteed to kill lavender, apart from a particularly bad frost, and that is bad drainage. It prefers a chalky soil, but can grow quite happily in sand, and most of the available species, although they hail from the Mediterranean, are hardy in Britain, particularly in the south. The most widely grown species is the common lavender (*L. angustifolia*), which is available in a huge range of cultivars, including white, pink and deep blue forms. It is an evergreen sub-shrub, with greyish-green leaves – both the leaves and the flowers have the characteristic lavender aroma. Also popular is the French lavender (*L. stoechas*), which has unusual tufted flower heads. It is not always winter hardy, but on well-drained soil it should survive. Lavenders can also be grown as low hedges and should be planted 30 cm (12 in) apart. Trim off straggly flower-heads in spring.

Lavender needs a light, sandy soil and really good drainage

PERENNIALS FOR THE DRY GARDEN

The sea holly (*Eryngium maritimum*) was once a common sight on the sandy beaches and fine shingle coasts of Britain, but it is gradually losing its habitat, partly due to natural erosion but also to the demands of tourism and development. Despite its natural defence mechanisms – leathery, spiny foliage to conserve moisture and to discourage predators, plus a long tap-root that can store water for days – it is not widespread in the

ABOVE: *Cultivated sea hollies* (Eryngium spp.) *thrive in dry gardens*
ABOVE RIGHT: *Thrift or sea pink* (Armeria maritimum)

wild. Happily it has found favour in gardens where it has a long and illustrious history. *E. maritimum* was once highly prized for its aromatic roots. Gerard's *Herbal* of 1597 described how they were preserved in sugar and orange water and were supposed to restore vitality to the elderly. Shakespeare's Falstaff wishes for 'eringoes', a renowned aphrodisiac, as he makes his rendezvous with Mistress Ford in Windsor Forest. The trade in the candied root of sea holly flourished in Colchester, Essex, from around 1600 until the mid-nineteenth century. Several species other than the native *E. maritimum* were grown in Elizabethan gardens, including *E. planum* and *E. alpinum*.

Today's garden eryngiums are suitable for a dry, sunny spot on well-drained soil, where they will attract bees and butterflies to their thistly purple flower-heads in late summer. The native form is not the most elegant or the most colourful, and for a haze of blue, a species like *E. bourgatii*, a native of the Pyrenees, is a good choice, particularly the cultivar 'Oxford Blue'. Most species are perennial, but the form known as Miss Wilmott's Ghost (*E. x giganteum*) is a tall, statuesque biennial, which self-seeds itself happily around a dry garden. The story goes that Ellen Wilmott, a contemporary of Gertrude Jekyll, scattered the seed around various gardens, unbeknown to the owners. The first they knew of it was when it raised its silvery, almost ethereal silhouette, and they caught their first glimpse of it in the back lighting of a late summer evening.

Annual California poppies (Eschscholzia californica) will self-seed amongst the perennials

Perennial sea hollies can be grown from seed, which is available from seed merchants, or from small container-raised plants. Seed should be sown in autumn in pots of gritty compost and overwintered in a cold frame. Alternatively, root cuttings can be taken from the plant in winter and treated in the same way. Sea hollies positively thrive on poor soils and, in fact, if the soil is too rich, the stems will become soft and floppy and need staking.

Thrifts or sea pinks are widely grown and popular in gardens where the clumps of rose pink flowers flourish at the edge of paths, in rockeries or on sunny dry banks. They are resistant to salt, wind, drought and extremes of temperature, which makes them good for gardens on exposed sites, such as hillsides or high-rise developments. The native thrift (*Armeria maritima*) of coastal dunes, cliffs and mountains makes a good compact plant 20 cm (8 in) high by 50 cm (20 in) wide and is available in white and deep pink varieties, as well as the original mid-pink. The related *A. juniperifolia* has purple-pink flowers and will do well in a container. All thrifts need good drainage, and should be grown in a sandy or gritty soil or compost. Clip off the flower stalks after they have finished to keep the plant looking neat. In the right conditions thrift should flower from late spring until midsummer. To create more plants, simply divide the plants after flowering, replant and water them in immediately.

Stonecrops or sedums are typical plants of rocky, stony habitats and several of the wild plants have made a successful transition to the garden. The one most commonly seen on garden walls and roof tops is *Sedum acre*, the so-called biting stonecrop or wallpepper. The shoots have a bitter, peppery taste, hence the common names, and it can be found growing wild on shingle beaches and sand dunes. It is a mat-forming evergreen

perennial with bright yellow flowers in early summer, easy to establish in a stony or sandy soil, but it always looks better on a wall or bank, rather than prostrate on the ground. The English stonecrop (*Sedum anglicum*) is similar but the flowers are pinkish-white.

No seashore-style garden would be complete without one or more of the *Crambe* species. The most dramatic member of the family is the sea kale (*C. maritima*), which is grown both as an edible vegetable and as an ornamental plant. It has broad clusters of white flowers in early summer and huge sculptural, fleshy, dark blue-green leaves, which look stunning against a pale sandy background. As a vegetable, it is the young stems that are succulent and the traditional method of harvesting is to wait for the stems to appear in the spring, pile sand around them to blanch them and reduce some of the bitterness and then cut them for the table. They are boiled in water and eaten with butter like asparagus. Sadly, it was the harvesting of the wild plant in the nineteenth century that led to the decline of sea kale around the coasts, but it is quite acceptable to buy plants from a nursery and to raise it in the garden. Another member of the kale family is *C. cordifolia*, which bears resemblance to a giant gypsophila with clouds of starry white flowers on slender branching stems. *C. cordifolia* is a good ornamental plant for the dry garden but needs plenty of room to spread.

Slatted wooden decking and deck loungers fit the seaside planting perfectly

SELF-SEEDING ANNUALS
AND BIENNIALS

It is an integral part of the philosophy of wild gardening that we should look out for wild plants that seed themselves in the garden before we pull them up as weeds. It is worth trying to identify any wild plant that turns up, just to see which species would grow naturally in your particular garden microclimate. Even if the plant itself is unattractive, its occurrence might suggest other members of its plant group that might be happy in the same environment.

A seashore or dry garden can include lots of hardy annuals and biennials that will seed themselves around and give the garden a natural appearance. The plants to choose are those that have naturally adapted to seaside conditions. The yellow horned poppy (*Glaucium flavum*) found growing wild on shingle beaches and dunes is perfectly suited to a dry garden on poor soil. It is a biennial and the seeds are best sown *in situ*, where the seedlings will gradually build up into an impressive plant about 60 cm (2 ft) tall and 45 cm (18 in) wide with fleshy grey leaves and large, open-faced yellow flowers in summer. The most striking part of the plant is the seed pods, which are up to 30 cm (1 ft) long and shaped like a sickle or a horn. When they are ripe they split lengthways and shed the seeds, which should establish themselves around the garden for flowering the following year. There is also a red horned poppy (*G. corniculatum*) which is a native of southern Europe – it has smaller flowers but enjoys the same conditions.

Evening primroses (*Oenothera* species) like a well-drained sandy soil and a sunny position. The biennial *O. biennis* has fragrant yellow flowers from early summer to autumn and makes a tall, short-lived plant. It self-seeds prolifically, but can be easily weeded out if there are too many seedlings. *Lychnis flos-jovis*, the downy-leafed, pink-flowered catchfly, is actually a perennial but like the evening primrose will self-seed freely. Also good for a dry garden are the California poppies (*Eschscholzia californica*), available in a wide range of colours from pale yellow, orange, scarlet red and bronze. They are annuals and should be sown *in situ* and left undisturbed to self-seed.

BULBOUS PLANTS FOR THE DRY GARDEN

Bulbs are often associated with woodland settings and cool, shady gardens, but several bulb species flourish in the hot, well-drained environment of the seashore garden. Agapanthus from South Africa are not always hardy in British gardens, but they have more chance of survival in a light, sandy soil, which doesn't get waterlogged. They are wonderful bold summer flowers, with tall stems and a crown of vivid blue tubular flowers, which give way to attractive seed-heads that can be left on the plant. The hardiest group is the Headbourne hybrids but the species *Agapanthus campanulatus* is also worth trying. Cultivars and hybrids offer a range of colours from white to dark blue and all shades in between. Technically, agapanthus is a fleshy-rooted perennial rather than a bulb and the crowns should be set about 5 cm (2 in) below soil level in April or May. Agapanthus also grow well in pots, as long as they are given a good drainage layer.

Crocosmia species can be included in the seashore garden to add a splash of bright colour in late summer and autumn. Like agapanthus, crocosmia are natives of South Africa and like well-drained soil, and although they prefer regular watering in the summer are quite tolerant of short periods of drought. The iris-like leaves form substantial clumps and produce funnel-shaped flowers in shades of red, yellow and orange. They are hardy in most winters, although prolonged frost can kill them. Montbretia (*C.* x *crocosmiiflora*) has naturalized itself on sea cliffs around Britain and in the garden it can be invasive, although it is quite easy to dig up overgrown clumps to keep it under control. There are lots of garden cultivars, varying in height from 45 cm (18 in) to 1 m (3 ft). A particularly bold variety is 'Lucifer', which, as its name suggests, has flaming red flowers and reaches over 1 m (3 ft) high. Crocosmia corms should be planted 7.5 cm (3 in) deep in late winter or early spring. After flowering, allow the leaves to die back naturally as this enables the plant to build up food reserves. Overcrowded clumps that have stopped flowering can be divided in the spring.

Crambe cordifolia, a relative of the wild seakale with rose campion (Lychnis coronaria)

SEASHORE GARDEN PLANTS

	HEIGHT X SPREAD

Sea Holly (*Eryngium maritimum*) — 50 cm (20 in) x 50 cm (20 in)
Spiny blue-grey foliage; small silver-blue flower-heads, July/August; evergreen perennial

Eryngium bourgatii — 60 cm (24 in) x 50 cm (20 in)
Grey-green foliage; blue stems; rounded lilac-blue flower-heads, July/August; herbaceous perennial

Eryngium planum — 75 cm (2 ft 6 in) x 45 cm (18 in)
Dark green foliage; deep blue flower heads, July/August; evergreen perennial

Eryngium alpinum — 1 m (3 ft) x 60 cm (2 ft)
Glossy deep green foliage; purple-blue flower heads, July/August; herbaceous perennial

Eryngium x *giganteum* (Miss Willmott's Ghost) — 1.2 m (4 ft) x 60 cm (2 ft)
Deep green foliage; silvery bracts; blue flower heads, July/August; biennial

Yellow Horned Poppy (*Glaucium flavum*) — 60 cm (2 ft) x 30 cm (1 ft)
Bristly blue-green leaves; bright yellow poppy-like flowers, July; biennial

Red Horned Poppy (*Glaucium corniculatum*) — 45 cm (18 in) x 30 cm (12 in)
Grey-green leaves; red or orange flowers, June; annual

Thrift or Sea Pink (*Armeria maritima*) — 23 cm (9 in) x 45 cm (18 in)
Narrow, grass-like leaves; pink globe-shaped flower-heads, May to August; evergreen perennial

Armeria juniperifolia — 25 cm (10 in) x 25 cm (10 in)
Grey-green linear leaves; purple-pink flower-heads, May to July; evergreen perennial

Sea-kale (*Crambe maritima*) — 75 cm (2 ft 6 in) x 1 m (3 ft)
Large, fleshy blue-green leaves; white flower-heads, June; perennial

Crambe cordifolia — 2.4 m (8 ft) x 1.5 m (5 ft)
Glossy green leaves; white starry flowers, May to July; perennial

Biting Stonecrop (*Sedum acre*) — 5 cm (2 in) x 15 cm (6 in)
Mat-forming succulent foliage; bright yellow flowers, May to July; evergreen perennial. Note: Sap can cause skin irritation.

California Poppy (*Eschscholzia californica*) — 35 cm (14 in) x 20 cm (8 in)
Grey-green foliage; yellow or orange poppy-like flowers, June to August; annual

Lychnis flos-jovis — 45 cm (18 in) x 45 cm (18 in)
Downy leaves and stems; rose-pink flowers, June to August; herbaceous perennial

Evening Primrose (*Oenothera biennis*) — 1 m (40 in) x 40 cm (16 in)
Lance-shaped leaves with red veins; yellow scented flowers, June to September; biennial

Agapanthus Headbourne Hybrids — 1 m (40 in) x 45 cm (18 in)
Strap-shaped leaves, tall stems topped with blue flowers, August; fleshy-rooted perennial

Agapanthus campanulatus — 1.2 m (4 ft) x 45 cm (18 in)
Narrow grey-green leaves; tall stems with soft blue flowers, August; fleshy-rooted perennial

Montbretia (*Crocosmia* x *crocosmiiflora*)   1 m (3 ft) x variable
Narrow, grass-like leaves; small orange flower spikes, August/September; perennial corm

Crocosmia 'Lucifer'   1.1 m (40 in) x variable
Strap-shaped leaves; scarlet flowers, August/September; perennial corm

English Lavender (*Lavandula angustifolia*)   60 cm (2 ft) x 60 cm (2 ft)
Grey-green aromatic leaves; fragrant blue flower spikes, July/August; evergreen shrub

French Lavender (*Lavandula stoechas*)   45 cm (12 in) x 45 cm (12 in)
Silvery-grey aromatic leaves; fragrant purple tufted flower-heads, July to September; evergreen shrub

SEASHORE GARDEN SHRUBS

Sea Buckthorn (*Hippophäe rhamnoides*)   2-4 m (6–12 ft) x 2m (6 ft)
Linear silvery leaves; spiny branches; orange berries, July/August; evergreen

Elaeagnus pungens 'Maculata'   2–3 m (6–10 ft) x 1.2 m (4 ft)
Dark green leaves with central gold blotch; small fragrant white flowers, October; evergreen

Elaeagnus pungens 'Frederici'   2–3 m (6–10 ft) x 1.2 m (4 ft)
Pale yellow leaves with green margin; small fragrant white flowers, October; evergreen

Tree Purslane (*Atriplex halimus*)   1–2.4 m (3–8 ft) x 1.2 m (4 ft)
Silvery grey leaves; semi-evergreen

Tamarisk (*Tamarix gallica*)   1–3 m (3–9 ft) x 2 m (6 ft)
Fine, feathery grey-green leaves; dark purple bark; pink flower racemes, July to September; deciduous

Tamarix tetranda   4 m (12 ft) x 4 m (12 ft)
Feathery pale green foliage, pink flower sprays, April to June; deciduous

Escallonia 'Apple Blossom'   1.5 m (5 ft) x 1 m (3 ft)
Glossy green leaves; pink and white flowers, May to September intermittently; evergreen

Escallonia rubra var. *macrantha*   3 m (9 ft) x 1.5 m (5 ft)
Glossy green aromatic leaves; deep rosy red flowers, May to September intermittently; evergreen

Burnet rose (*Rosa pimpinellifolia*)   1 m (3 ft) x 1.2 m (4 ft)
Thorny stems; small grey-green leaves; single white flowers, June; deciduous

Tree Mallow (*Lavatera* 'Barnsley')   2 m (6 ft) x 1.5 m (5 ft)
Downy grey-green leaves; white flowers with pink eye, July to October; semi-evergreen

Lavatera 'Candy Floss'   2 m (6 ft) x 1.5 m (5 ft)
Downy grey-green leaves; sugar pink flowers, July to October; semi-evergreen

Lavatera maritima   1 m (3 ft) x 30 cm (12 in)
Downy grey-green leaves; pink flowers with darker veins, July to September; semi-evergreen

Daisy Bush (*Olearia* x *haastii*)   2 m (6 ft) x 1 m (3 ft)
Grey-green leaves; scented white daisy-like flowers, July/August; evergreen

SEASHORE WILDLIFE

The seashore habitat is alive with the cries of wading birds feeding on the huge numbers of invertebrates that live in the sand. This is the haunt of curlews, redshanks, oyster-catchers and knots that probe the mud for snails, lugworms and ragworms. Where the beach meets the cliff sandmartins will build their nests in the soft sandstone or chalk. On harder granite cliffs seabirds nest on ledges, jutting out precariously high above the seashore. Here, herring gulls breed, along with colonies of kittiwakes, guillemots and razorbills. On the beach itself, visiting little terns insist on making their nests in the most exposed positions among the shingle: many nature reserves rope off their breeding areas from the public during the summer.

Where there are plants on the shoreline there will also be butterflies, like the large skipper, which as its name suggests 'skips' from plant to plant in high summer, taking nectar from sea hollies and sea asters and laying its eggs on dune grasses. Less conspicuous, but very common on sandy shorelines, is the grayling, a perfectly camouflaged butterfly whose mottled yellow and brown colouring makes it almost impossible to see against a background of sand or shingle. Meadow browns, small heaths and ringlets may also be spotted at the coast, particularly if there are enough grasses for the caterpillars to feed on. Where the coastline is heavily populated, common garden butterflies, like tortoiseshells, will extend their range of flight down to the beach. In the Isle of Wight a rare butterfly known as Glanville's fritillary may sometimes be seen. It is named after Eleanor Glanville, a butterfly enthusiast of the eighteenth century, and inhabits the coastal chalk cliffs.

Many of the typical plants grown in a 'seashore' garden will attract a wide range of wildlife. Lavender, thyme and thrift

Lulworth Cove, Dorset

are attractive to bees. Both native and non-native forms of sea holly are a magnet to bees and butterflies in late summer. Evening primroses rely on moths for their pollination, and as the light fades moths are guided to the nectar in the plant by the pale colour and light scent. Hebes, rock roses, tree mallows and escallonias all have good, easily accessible flowers for bees and butterflies. Plants like the horned poppy rely on bees and other flying insects for their pollination.

One of the benefits of this kind of garden is that there are very few pests – these silver-leaved and waxy-coated plants resist attack by slugs, which find it difficult anyway to crawl over shingle or sand. However, attracting some local birds into the garden will help to keep any pests under control. Because a seashore garden is a by nature a 'dry' garden, it is worth including some dishes of water for visiting birds.

WHERE TO SEE...
SEASHORE AND SEASHORE PLANTS

Britain has an extensive coastline and seashore habitats are within reach of most population centres. The National Trust owns substantial areas of coast in Wales and England, and local councils are responsible for many more stretches. The contacts given here are just a selection of the many thousands of miles of seashore waiting to be explored.

SAND DUNES AND SAND DUNE FLORA

Braunton Burrows
North Devon coast, 6 miles north-west of Barnstaple – probably the best location to see a great diversity of flora. Privately owned, but open to the public throughout the year.

Kenfig National Nature Reserve
Ton Kenfig, Pyle, Mid Glamorgan CF33 4PT, telephone 01656 743386.

Sefton coast, Merseyside
Sefton Metropolitan Borough Council, Leisure Services Department, Coast and Countryside Management Services, Formby Council Offices, Freshfield Road, Formby L37 3PG, telephone 0151 934 2959.
Additional information about the coast and the Sefton Coast Life Project is also available on the website http://www.merseyworld.com/sclife.

SHINGLE BEACH AND SHINGLE FLORA

Snettisham Beach, Norfolk
Partly owned by the RSPB, telephone 01485 542689, and partly by the Borough Council of King's Lynn and West Norfolk, Valentine Road, Hunstanton Norfolk PE36 SE2, telephone 01553 692722.

Chesil Beach
Chesil Bank and the Fleet Nature Reserve
The Royal Manor of Portland, Chesil Beach Centre, Portland, Dorset DT4 9XE, telephone 01305 760579.

Orford Ness, Suffolk
The National Trust (Quay Office), Orford Quay, Orford, Woodbridge, Suffolk IP12 2NU.
Includes shingle, salt marsh and mud-flat habitats.

CLIFFS AND CLIFF-TOP FLORA

Studland
For details of the cliff-top walk contact the Countryside Office (NT), Middle Beach, Studland, Swanage, Dorset BH19 3AX, telephone 01929 450259.

Portland Bill, Dorset
The Visitors' Centre (including the Tourist Information Centre) is situated in front of the lighthouse at Portland Bill; permanent exhibitions and visits to the lighthouse. Details of local events can be obtained from the Weymouth and Portland Borough Council, telephone 01305 761222.

Chapter 5

Hedg

erow

HEDGES HAVE BEEN AN INTEGRAL PART of the British landscape for thousands of years. They are among the oldest visible man-made features, used for marking boundaries, enclosing settlements, protecting livestock and providing fuel and food. They give character to the countryside and provide wildlife corridors for plants, mammals, birds and insects. However, in the last fifty years we have lost half of the pre-war 600,000 kilometres (375,000 miles) of hedgerows. Intensive farming and urban development have accounted for most of the losses and it is estimated that each year another 18,000 kilometres (11,250 miles) disappear. It is because we are losing our hedgerows at such at alarming rate that it has become vital to preserve existing garden hedgerows and to plant new ones. In the garden, hedges can provide the nesting sites, food and shelter for wildlife that are missing from the countryside.

As with many landscape features, hedges occur in every period of human settlement from prehistoric times onwards. Evidence of hedging plants, such as hawthorn and blackthorn, has been found in association with Roman sites in Oxfordshire. The Anglo-Saxons certainly planted mixed hedges and in Old English hawthorn simply means hedge-thorn, which suggests that it was a common hedging shrub. Hedges were planted, replanted, laid and managed throughout the Middle Ages, but the greatest period of hedge planting was as result of the Enclosure Acts. Between 1700 and 1850, approximately 320,000 kilometres (200,000 miles) of hedges were planted to mark and divide up areas that had been common land or had been farmed under the open field system. For economy and convenience the 'new' hedges were mainly single species, usually hawthorn, and can be identified by their straight lines and uniform appearance. They are quite different from the pre-1700 hedges, which tend to include a random mix of species, such as blackthorn, elm, field maple, hawthorn, dogwood, ash, dog rose and elder. They may also contain a number of old trees or stools of former trees, and tend to meander, following curved boundaries, old lanes and even watercourses.

HOW OLD IS A HEDGE?

This is a question that has absorbed and delighted historians and ecologists for many years and which has, naturally, no easy answer. One theory, known as Hooper's Rule, suggests that a hedge can be dated by the number of species that appear in a given length of it, 30 m (90 ft) – the more species, the older the hedge. One species is supposed to represent a hundred years, so a hedge with seven species would be seven hundred years old. This is quite a fun exercise to do with local hedges, but unless you have some documented evidence of when a hedge was first planted, it is difficult to prove conclusively.

Most hedges have arisen from deliberate human planting but they occasionally spring up naturally along man-made barriers, such as wires or fences, perhaps because birds have sat on the fence and dropped seeds, which then grow under the protection of the barrier. Some hedges represent the remnants of former woodland. When a wood is grubbed up or felled, it is quite usual to leave a border 'hedge' as the boundary of the newly created field. These woodland hedges contain species that would not normally

occur in a planted hedge, perhaps full-size oak and elm trees which, although they do occur in planted hedges, are less common than in proper woodland. More indicative is the presence of small-leafed lime (*Tilia cordata*) or the service tree (*Sorbus torminalis*), which are woodland trees not hedging shrubs. Woodland flowers, like dog's mercury, bluebells and wood anemones, can also indicate former woodland.

Informal boundary hedges help to make a natural transition from the garden to the wider landscape

HEDGEROW ECONOMIES

In areas of the country where woodland was sparse, hedges were and still are important suppliers of woodland products. It was quite common practice to leave 'standard' trees at regular intervals along the length of a hedge, which would either be allowed to grow up into a full tree for timber, or be coppiced and pollarded to supply poles for fencing and fuel. Even where woodland was common, hedges were important for keeping livestock in check – the thornier the better.

Once planted a hedge needed management, mainly in the process of laying or 'plashing', a skilled practice carried out whenever it became gappy around the base. The individual stems or trunks are sliced three-quarters through near the base and laid horizontally on the ground so that new growth springs up. This makes the bottom of the hedge thick and impenetrable and encourages lots of new growth further up. Hedge laying and hand trimming are still practised in rural areas, but are far less common than the practice of cutting hedges with huge mechanical trimmers which tear the branches indiscriminately.

Hedges have also provided treasure trove for local people. In medieval times hedge stealing was commonplace and those who stole wood or thorn 'sets' (young plants)

The golden-leaved bramble (Rubus cockburnianus 'Golden Vale') grows to about 1.8m (6ft) and is not as invasive as the wild bramble

from their lord's hedge were heavily fined. Hedges were not wild, but were owned and managed. Nevertheless, the gathering of autumn fruit from the hedgerows to supplement a meagre diet has been a long-held tradition. Rosehips, elderberries, blackberries, sloes, haws and crab apples were, and still are, collected for the kitchen, and recipes for the wild bounty are handed down from generation to generation.

THE GARDEN HEDGEROW

Many gardens already include a hedge but more often than not they are monocultures, containing only one species such as privet, laurel, yew or Leyland cypress. Although these evergreen, single-species hedges are useful for sheltering the garden and for bird nesting, they are limited in the diversity of plant and animal life they can support. If it is not practical to take out or change a hedge like this, it can still be improved by introducing climbing plants to grow through its foliage or by introducing a richer planting in front of it. If you wish to put in a new hedge it is always worth taking a look at local 'wild' hedgerows to see how they are planted and what species they contain. As well as the shrubs, there may be trees, climbers and hedgerow flowers, and a mix of deciduous and evergreen species. By including a thorny species like hawthorn, an evergreen like holly and four or five others, which flower and fruit at different times, the hedge will be a richer and more interesting habitat while still serving its purpose of screening your garden from the neighbours.

Planting a climbing rose to grow through a single-species hedge will make it richer in flowers and fruit

CHOOSING HEDGING SHRUBS

Native species should be the first choice, simply because they support a greater range of wildlife and will give the garden a more natural appearance. Consider whether you really need to keep the hedge neatly clipped: if you do, there will not be the abundance of flowers and fruit that an unclipped hedge provides. A compromise might be to leave it growing freely during the spring and summer and clip it once a year after the berries have finished. If your garden backs on to rough ground, hedges can be left to grow really high – to 3–4 m (9–12 ft) – to give the garden a secluded, protected feel.

HAWTHORN

The most popular deciduous hedging shrub has always been hawthorn. It makes a thorny, fairly impenetrable barrier and can either be clipped neatly or left to grow freely for a more informal effect. It grows at a medium pace (slower than privet, but quicker than yew or holly) and you could expect new plants to form a fairly dense hedge in four or five years. Hawthorn (*Crataegus monogyna*) has lots of affectionate country names: in Somerset and Hampshire it is known as the bread-and-cheese bush and in Shropshire as the hipperty-haw tree. The young leaves have a nutty flavour and can be eaten in sandwiches, hence 'bread and cheese', and were picked off the tree and eaten by children as they walked along country lanes. Many counties know it as whitethorn or may. The creamy white blossom with its distinctive smell is a sure sign that spring has arrived. In autumn the bright red berries or haws are traditionally made into a vitamin C rich jelly.

Dog rose (Rosa canina)
and variegated periwinkle
(Vinca major 'Variegata')
growing through a mature
hawthorn hedge

BLACKTHORN

Before the enclosures of the eighteenth and nineteenth centuries, when hawthorn was planted in huge quantities, blackthorn (*Prunus spinosa*) was a far more popular hedging shrub than it is today. It flowers earlier than the hawthorn, in February or March, and

even though the flowers are fairly inconspicuous they are useful for insects waking early from hibernation. It really comes into its own later in the year with a crop of sloes, small blue-black fruit, which are unpleasantly acidic if eaten fresh but make excellent sloe gin, wine and 'cheese', a rich preserve. The wild plum or bullace (*Prunus domestica*) is also found in hedges and has edible plums.

FIELD MAPLE

Acer campestre, the field or hedge maple, is also a constituent of old hedgerows in southern parts of Britain, and has tightly packed small green leaves that turn yellow in autumn before they fall. It also produces sycamore-type winged seeds that twirl and flutter to the ground. If left as a tree, it will form a round-headed specimen about 3–4 m (9–12 ft) high, and isolated specimens can still be found standing in the middle of a field. Maple was regularly coppiced from hedges and woods and, because the wood could be worked so thinly without splitting, it was used for inlaying furniture and to make musical instruments. Field maples have given their names to places such as Mapledurham in Oxfordshire and Maplebeck in Nottinghamshire.

DOGWOOD

Most people's picture of dogwood is of one of the ornamental species that are cut down annually to produce the attractive red stems in winter. In fact, the native dogwood, *Cornus sanguinea*, has the same attributes, with the red stems being most conspicuous in winter when the leaves have dropped. They turn a deep burgundy colour in autumn. The wood is very hard, and was used to make skewers, arrows and pipe stems. Dogwood grows best on chalky soils.

BUCKTHORN AND ALDER BUCKTHORN

Buckthorn (*Rhamnus catharticus*) is often found in old hedgerows, although it is rarely grown in gardens. It is a deciduous shrub with distinctive sharp spines at the end of the branches and bunches of black berries in autumn. The berries are poisonous, but they were collected by local people and delivered to chemists where they were turned into syrup of buckthorn – well known as a medicinal purge.

*Autumn berries of the guelder rose (*Viburnum opulus*)*

On damp ground, hedges often contain alder buckthorn (*Frangula alnus*), so called because the young leaves resemble alder leaves, being downy underneath, and because it enjoys similar damp conditions. It does not have the buckthorn's spines, but the berries are similar, although they turn red before black, while those of the buckthorn go straight from green to black. Alder buckthorn wood was reputed to produce the finest charcoal for making gunpowder.

HAZEL

The hazel or cobnut (*Corylus avellana*) was not a major component of ancient hedgerows but one or two shrubs or trees would have been found in the average hedge. It was more usually grown as a small coppiced tree in open woodland, where the flexible 'wands' would be cut and used for basket making and fencing. It can be included in a mixed garden hedge, where it will provide autumn nuts for squirrels and small mammals. The hazel usually cultivated for nuts is a different species, *Corylus maxima* (filbert), which gives a better crop.

ELDER

Elder (*Sambucus nigra*) is the most opportunist of hedging species and appears wherever there is a gap in a hedgerow. Many hedgerow elders may not have been deliberately planted, but have simply seeded themselves. It is useful for the garden because it is quick growing and has good blossom and berries. The frothy white summer flowers are cut and collected for elderflower cordials and eaten fried in pancakes, while the black, juicy autumn berries are made into wine and preserves – although they are toxic when eaten raw. The berries are also excellent for blackbirds and thrushes.

HEDGING ROSES

The rose most commonly found in hedges is the dog rose (*Rosa canina*), with its arching stems and small pinkish-white flowers. This looks good in tall, natural-looking hedges, but for impenetrability it might be better to go for the sweet briar (*R. rubiginosa*), a more compact plant with deeper pink flowers. Sweet briar takes its name not so much from the perfume of the flowers but from the leaves, which give off a delicious fresh aroma after rain or when they are crushed. The hips from both these wild roses were collected and made into syrup – an important source of vitamin C before citrus fruits were widely available. Of the garden roses, *R. rugosa* is widely sold for hedging and has showy flowers and huge hips. The cultivar 'Roseraie de l'Hay' has wine-red flowers with a good perfume, and creates a really dense, thorny bush. Rugosas could be substituted for the wild roses, particularly if they are grown mixed in with other species rather than in a single row. Any of the rambling roses such as 'Seagull' or 'Félicité Perpétue' can be grown through a hedge where they will scramble up to the light and produce flowers at the top.

EVERGREENS

It is worth including one or two evergreens within the hedge, to give some winter cover for birds and to support a few specific insects. Holly (*Ilex aquifolium*) is a good choice, making a prickly barrier which keeps out people but allows birds a safe nesting site and supports the holly blue butterfly. Holly is slow growing but will eventually produce wonderful winter berries. The wild privet (*Ligustrum vulgare*) is not fully evergreen like the garden privet, but it was an old hedgerow shrub and has many dependent insects, such as the privet hawk moth. Native box (*Buxus sempervirens*) is another evergreen shrub that is rarely allowed to grow freely in a hedge but is more usually clipped into formal shapes. It is a natural inhabitant of open beech woods and scrubland on chalky soils but is now found in only a few localities in the southern counties of Britain, including Kent and Buckinghamshire. It grows happily, if very slowly, in a mixed garden hedge, reaching 3–4 m (9–12 ft) eventually.

CLIMBERS AND FILLERS

A walk along an old hedgerow will confirm that there is much more to it than its shrubs. Climbing through the dense network of twigs will be ivy, wild honeysuckle, clematis and wild blackberry, and all help to give the hedge its individual character. The ivy (*Hedera helix*), with its leathery green leaves, weaves its way to the outer edges where it gives the hedge an evergreen appearance in winter. Its dense clumps produce umbels of yellow, nectar-rich flowers in autumn, which are a magnet to bees, other insects and butterflies. The wild honeysuckle (*Lonicera periclymenum*), with its creamy yellow flowers in late summer, looks so much better left to scramble through a hedge than trained unnaturally against trellis. Clematis (*Clematis vitalba*) is grown mainly for its fluffy white seed-heads,

which provoked its country name, old man's beard. Both the wild honeysuckle and the clematis can be rampant, so if the hedge is small, be prepared for them to take off into nearby trees, or even a neighbour's garden, in search of light. Bramble or wild blackberry can't be recommended for the garden even though it has wonderful fruit and flowers: once introduced it is virtually impossible to remove.

Taxus baccata 'Lutea' (a cultivated form of the common yew) makes a slow-growing evergreen hedge

NATIVE HEDGING SHRUBS

NB: Heights given are for hedges left to grow naturally, but they will stay more compact if trimmed regularly. Likewise, many will reach heights of at least double those given, if grown as a tree.

E$^{\bullet}$=evergreen

	HEIGHT
Alder buckthorn (*Frangula alnus*) *Berries (toxic)*	4 m (12 ft)
Blackthorn (*Prunus spinosa*) *Blossom, sloes*	3 m (9 ft)
Box (E$^{\bullet}$) (*Buxus sempervirens*) *All-year-round foliage*	5 m (15 ft)
Buckthorn (*Rhamnus catharticus*) *Berries (toxic)*	6 m (18 ft)
Crab Apple (*Malus sylvestris*) *Blossom, fruit*	5 m (15 ft)
Dogwood (*Cornus sanguinea*) *Autumn/winter colour*	4 m (12 ft)
Elder (*Sambucus nigra*) *Flowers, berries (toxic when raw)*	3–5 m (9–15 ft)
Field maple (*Acer campestre*) *Winged fruits*	6 m (18 ft)
Guelder rose (*Viburnum opulus*) *Flower, berries (toxic)*	4 m (12 ft)
Hawthorn (*Crataegus monogyna*) *Flowers, berries (haws)*	4 m (12 ft)
Hazel (*Corylus avellana*) *Autumn nuts*	5 m (15 ft)
Holly (E$^{\bullet}$) (*Ilex aquifolium*) *Berries (toxic)*	5 m (15 ft)
Rowan (*Sorbus aucuparia*) *Flowers, berries (toxic)*	4 m (12 ft)
Sweet Briar (*Rosa rubiginosa*) *Flowers, hips, scent*	3 m (9 ft)
Wayfaring Tree (*Viburnum lantana*) *Flowers, berries (toxic)*	4–6 m (12–18 ft)
Wild Cherry (*Prunus avium*) *Blossom, fruit (bitter, non-edible)*	6 m (18 ft)
Yew (*Taxus baccata*) *Berries (toxic)*	4 m (12 ft)

PLANTING A GARDEN HEDGE

A hedge does not have to be in a straight line. It can be gently curved or it can meander to follow the line of your boundary. Hedges can also be planted to divide up different parts of the garden, perhaps to separate the vegetable patch from the

A plain beech hedge, with climbing honeysuckle and Clematis *'Bill Mackenzie'*

flower borders. If you need access through the middle of the hedge, leave a space approximately 1 m (3 ft) wide when planting. A hedge can be planted either with one row of shrubs or, for extra protection, with two parallel rows, which will grow together to form a really impenetrable barrier. The choice of site depends on what will work and be practical in the garden, although hedging shrubs won't thrive on very wet ground. Hedges can be planted in front of a fence, but if it is a solid panel type it will eventually have to be taken down to allow light to that side of the hedge. The best time for hedge planting is in autumn or early spring, although container-grown plants can be put in at any time as long as the earth is not frozen or waterlogged; it is also best to avoid midsummer, when the heat will take its toll on the new plants.

◆ Mark out the line of the hedge using canes and string. Dig a trench in front of this line, about 60 cm (2 ft) wide and 45 cm (18 in) deep.

◆ Prepare the ground thoroughly by digging and removing all perennial weed roots. Add some garden compost or well-rotted manure and mix this with the loose soil at the base of the trench.

◆ Use two-year-old hedging plants (about 30–45 cm/12–18 in) high. Set the plants 30–45 cm (12–18 in) apart, making sure they are planted at the same depth as they were at the nursery. To be sure of this, line up the soil mark on the stem with the final soil level of the trench. Fill in around the roots with the excavated soil, firming down well.

◆ Water the plants thoroughly after planting, and regularly while they are getting established, particularly in the first year after planting. Keep any competing weeds at bay, particularly bindweed which in summer can twist itself around new plants and choke them. If you need to weed heavily take care not to dislodge the shrubs, firming them back down again afterwards. Mulching around the plants helps to deter weeds and keeps the moisture around the roots. It will also make a good environment for hedgerow plants.

MAINTAINING THE HEDGE

Cut back the central growing stem and side growths by about a third after planting. Do this every spring in the first few years to encourage bushy growth. Don't let the central stem get to its final height for at least two to three years: it is better to keep cutting back until the hedge has developed a strong framework of growth. A good height to aim for eventually is 1.2–1.5 m (4–5 ft), but it is quite possible to let hedges grow more freely up to 2.2–2.5 m (7–8 ft). After this height they are more difficult to manage.

Once the hedge is established you can start to manage it in a way that will give a more natural appearance and benefit wildlife. Usually garden hedges are clipped regularly, even weekly through the summer, but it is far better to give the hedge one trim a year, in late autumn when the hips and berries have finished and nesting is over. An alternative is occasionally to coppice individual species (elder, dogwood, oak and hazel respond well to this, see p. 28). Hedgelaying is the traditional way to restore old hedges (p. 127). It is a skilled craft, but if you have an extensive length of native hedge, it might be worth seeing if there are local craftspeople who will undertake it, or better still, take a course with a conservation organization and do the job yourself.

ROAD VERGES

Many people's first glimpse of a wild flower is through a car window, and whether we like it or not, the motor car is the most practical way for most of us to get out into the countryside and see wildflowers growing in their natural habitats. A haze of pink or purple rosebay willowherb on a motorway cutting, a bank of cowslips on a trunk road, or a strip of poppies by the side of a country lane – these are the sights that make us want to get out and explore further. Of course, there is so much more to be seen on foot or by bicycle than from a car window, but roadsides make a good first port of call for the amateur botanist and can be endless fascinating.

Road verges are a habitat in their own right and have their own ecology and flora. In towns and villages, verges have a long history of use, as convenient places to graze cattle and horses and even for haymaking. Depending on the prevailing climate, soil and situation, a verge can be a mini-meadow, a woodland edge, a hedgerow, a ditch or a wetland, or a small area of moorland or heath. We should never take our roadsides for granted, for in them we may have the survival of those habitats that have been lost from the surrounding area, to forestry plantations, to arable crops or to building developments.

No two road verges are the same. Some are fragments of the habitats mentioned above, but others have a distinct combination of plants that don't occur anywhere else. At first glance a road verge can look unpromising – all grass and cow parsley – but closer

inspection will reveal hundreds of wild plants that reflect the soil, the aspect and the history of that site. Mostly we find common species, but often they are plants that are local to a particular area and, occasionally, may be rare or endangered.

It is worthwhile studying a local verge for a full year, noting what plants appear in each season. This is where we might find many of the beleaguered meadow plants, like scabious, knapweeds and ox-eye daisies, or woodland plants, like helleborines, which have clung to their habitat in fragile clumps and have been joined by more boisterous colonizers like the umbellifers and ragworts.

Road verges like this one in north-west Norfolk are rich in wild plant species

Two very different verges in the north-west of Norfolk will serve to illustrate how roadsides reflect the diversity of the local flora. The first is an old lane that now divides a pine plantation from a huge barley field. The verges here are large, around 4 m (12 ft) wide, and until thirty years ago were used to graze cattle on their journeys between fields. The soil is light, almost pure sand, and as there is no hedge, the verge is open to the elements and has taken on a mini-heathland character with grasses, ragweed, harebells and thistles. In late summer it buzzes with cinnabar moths, grasshoppers and bees. It is in distinct contrast to the dark, cool pine forest only yards away – and to the heavily fertilized arable field on the other side.

Just three miles away, another village lane runs between a cabbage field and a newly planted orchard. Here, there are high old hedges on both sides, containing blackthorn and hawthorn, hazel and elder. The character of the verge is part-hedgerow–part-meadow, with meadow refuges like slender knapweed, chamomile,

ox-eye daisies and bird's foot trefoil growing alongside more typical hedgerow or verge plants, such as cow parsley, greater willowherb and purple tufted vetch.

All over Britain there are verges like these that have not been 'landscaped' or planted and are remnants of original habitats. However, over the past fifty years new roads and highways have been cut across the countryside and many verges have been seeded with amenity grasses and planted with young trees. The problem with most verges is that local authorities 'maintain' them and that means mowing them down. While this undoubtedly makes them look neater, and is often done for safety reasons, the flowers never get a chance to set seed and the verges soon become swamped by tougher grass.

Verges are usually the property of the Highways Authority, but are managed by the county councils. In some areas budgetary restrictions have meant that they are cut less often, which is good news for wildflowers. Some councils are even managing their verges for wildflowers, sowing new ones with a seed mixture of 80 per cent native grasses and 20 per cent wildflowers. Local people are beginning to realize that if the verges are not mown regularly they do not look uncared-for. Mowing later, after the flowers have set seed, gives species a chance to colonize and spread. Of course, not all verges are suitable for the hay meadow treatment, and consideration needs to be given to the subtle variations in the underlying bedrock, soil type, aspect and degree of shade. But all the signs show that forward-thinking authorities can appoint caretakers who understand these variations, and in future many more of our road verges may be full of woodland, wetland, meadow or heathland flowers.

HEDGEROW PLANTS

'Our wildflowers take possession
of the hedges that seam the land,
draping them with inimitable grace.'

WILLIAM ROBINSON,
THE WILD GARDEN, 1870

William Robinson was a great believer in hedges, which he called 'living fences'. He was scathing of the Victorian passion for iron railings which 'bid fair to ruin the beauty of the English landscape'. An iron fence, he said, gives neither protection nor privacy, requires too much 'tinkering' – maintenance – and should, wherever possible, be replaced with a natural hedge. He was also an advocate of climbing plants, both wild and exotic, and suggested that wild clematis could be grown through the body of the hedge alongside jasmine, honeysuckle, everlasting peas, Virginia creeper and perennial tropaeolums. At the base of the hedge, he planted violas, periwinkles, speedwells, trilliums, narcissi, snowflakes, wild strawberries and cranesbills. Hedgebottoms can be notoriously difficult to plant, the soil often being poor and dry and the aspect shady and cool. This, of

Astrantias need a rich soil and light shade, and are grown here with the perennial climbing pea

course, depends on which way the hedge is facing and some gardens have a south-facing border in front of their hedge, which is more like a conventional sunny border than a hedgerow. In fact, most plants are not growing right under the hedge, but in front of it and will get sunlight for at least part of the day. The important thing is to assess the hedge to see how much sun the plants will get and plant accordingly. Hedging shrubs take a lot of nutrients and moisture from the soil, hence the dryness, and there are two ways of dealing with this: either use plants that can cope with the dry conditions or counteract the dryness by mulching the hedgerow every spring and autumn with garden compost, old mushroom compost or leaf mould. This is a good idea, anyway, particularly when the shrubs and plants are trying to establish themselves. If you are introducing new plants it is better to use pot-grown specimens, which already have a well-developed root system, rather than seedlings or plug plants which might struggle to survive in less than ideal conditions. Always water the plants thoroughly before and after planting. Young plants can be protected with home-made cloches, cut from clear plastic bottles, to guard against slug and animal damage.

The purple deadnettle

(Lamium orvala)

HEDGEBOTTOM PLANTS

Of the low-growing hedgerow plants, the deadnettles are probably the most useful summer-flowering species. They are often overlooked by gardeners in favour of more glamorous specimens, but they are tough groundcover plants for shady places. As the name suggests, they resemble nettles but have no sting. The white deadnettle (*Lamium album*) is perhaps the most coarse-looking of the bunch but it is excellent for bees, and where the soil is fairly fertile it will form a large patch. It is good for areas that are intended to look wild. The spotted deadnettle (*L. maculatum*) is more widely grown in gardens and has attractive mottled leaves and pink or purple flowers. There are several good garden cultivars, including 'White Nancy', which has pure white flowers. 'Beacon Silver' has almost completely silver leaves, which really light up a dark corner; it is lower growing than the other deadnettles, forming a carpet about 20 cm (8 in) high, and bears mauve-pink flowers in summer. Deadnettles need no fussing, although to get a good foliage cover, you can shear off the plants after flowering to encourage new leaf growth – this is not essential and they will grow quite well without any interference. If the plants are overgrowing their allotted space, they can be dug up and divided in spring or autumn – you can make new plants by replanting the rooted divisions.

Closely related to the deadnettles and often found growing in their company in the wild is betony (*Stachys officinalis*). The leaves are also nettle-like and the flowers are a really clear pink. Like the deadnettles, betony is a good groundcover plant, forming a mat of foliage from which the flower spikes emerge in midsummer. Betony has supernatural associations and was used by medieval herbalists in a potion to ward off evil spirits. It comes from the same family as the hedge woundwort (*Stachys sylvatica*), which has duller flowers but is otherwise quite similar and a wonderful bee plant.

Self-heals are traditional hedgerow plants that have transferred successfully to

the garden. The common self-heal (*Prunella vulgaris*) is a low-growing, spreading perennial with deep violet-blue flowers. *P. grandiflora* is commonly grown in gardens: it is larger flowered and available in a range of different-coloured cultivars, including 'Pink Loveliness', with soft pink flowers, and 'Loveliness', which is pale violet-blue. Self-heals do well in dry shade and the flower production is actually better on poor soils: on rich, fertile soils the foliage grows at the expense of the flowers. They start flowering in June and the blooms can last all summer. The name self-heal was adopted because the plant was used for treating wounds. In Somerset and Gloucester it is known as the carpenter's herb, perhaps because it was on hand every time the woodworker made a slip with the hammer or saw.

No hedgerow would be complete without *Arum maculatum*, known variously as white arum, lords-and-ladies or cuckoo-pint. It has two main seasons of interest: in spring, the bright green heart-shaped leaves appear and the plant produces a conspicuous purplish yellow spathe, rather like an unfolding handkerchief. Through the summer the plant is hardly noticeable, but in early autumn, the fruit spike appears with bright red or orange berries which are poisonous. Gardeners also grow the larger *A. italicum*, which has white-veined leaves and a cleaner, almost white spathe. Both are grown from tubers, which should be planted out in summer and covered with a mulch to prevent them drying out. Once established they will need no special care, although an annual mulch will help to retain moisture.

Periwinkles (*Vinca major* and *V. minor*) will thrive in the deep shade of the hedgebottom even if they don't produce as many flowers as they would in a sunnier position. The large periwinkle is very rampant but excellent if you need it to compete with tough weeds like ground elder. The smaller-leaved *Vinca minor* is better if you don't want the plant to spread. Both species are evergreen and available in variegated forms. Even in shade they will produce their pretty mauve or purple flowers intermittently over a long period, in mild years right up until November and then again in early spring.

Cuckoo pint or 'lords and ladies' (Arum maculatum)

HEDGEFRONT PLANTING

The area in front of the hedge offers the gardener lots of scope for planting. It may still be dry and shady, but it need not be lacking in flowers or colour. Two of the cranesbills are especially suited to shade, the lilac wood cranesbill (*Geranium sylvaticum*), which grows best on a slightly moist soil, and the pink hedgerow cranesbill (*G. pyrenaicum*) for dry soil. Cranesbills look pretty growing among stitchwort, either the lesser stitchwort (*Stellaria*

graminia) on light, chalky soils, or the larger-flowered greater stitchwort (*S. holostea*) on heavier or acid soils. Both plants are too lax and sprawling to look good on their own, but with cranesbills or red campion the effect is a delicate tapestry of colour from late spring into summer. If there is a place to put a small plant where it won't get swamped by other more vigorous plants, sweet woodruff (*Galium odoratum*) is

ABOVE LEFT: Geranium sanguineum *var.* striatum *with bell flowers* (campanula)
ABOVE: *Seed pods of honesty* (Lunaria annua)

pretty and thrives in well-drained soil with full or partial shade. It is low growing with bright green leaves and starry white flowers in late spring and early summer. If there is no competition, it will spread to form a good carpet and both the leaves and flowers have a sweet, hay-like scent. It could be grown with the annual herb robert (*Geranium robertianum*), which, once introduced, will self-seed each year. This also thrives on dry

LEFT: *White comfrey* (Symphytum orientale)
BOTTOM: Astrantia major *subsp.* involucrata *'Shaggy'*

ground and the ferny leaves and small pink and white striped flowers are delicate enough not to detract from the woodruff.

If the hedge is tall, the front planting could include some of the taller perennials, like sweet cicely (*Myrrhis odorata*), with its fern-like leaves and fluffy flowers which give way to aromatic black seed heads. It is a typical hedgerow and roadside plant, but it needs lots of space as it will spread to over 1 m (3 ft) wide and 2 m (6 ft) tall and new seedlings will spring up quite prolifically. Cow parsley (*Anthriscus sylvestris*) is similar in appearance although slightly shorter. The pink cow parsley (*Pimpinella major* 'Rosea') is a very pretty plant, but needs a sunny aspect. You could also introduce seed of honesty (*Lunaria annua*), which is biennial and can hold its own in many different growing conditions. The pretty purple summer flowers are followed by translucent, papery discs, which ripen and release masses of seed, ensuring that the flowers will return year after year.

The taller campanulas are excellent for planting in front of a hedge: they are tough and adaptable to shade or sun. The nettle-leafed bellflower (*Campanula trachelium*) is a tall perennial with rough, bristly leaves and large bell-shaped violet-blue flowers in late summer – good for a dryish soil. If the soil is moist, the giant bellflower (*C. latifolia*) would be a better choice and, given the right conditions, will form a substantial clump. It is similar to *C. trachelium* but does not have the bristly leaves. Both plants can be found in wild hedgerows, although they are quite scarce, and both are excellent for bees. The peach-leafed bellflower (*C. persicifolia*) is a more slender, delicate plant than the others mentioned here. It copes well with a dry soil and adapts to full sun or partial shade. The natural colour of bellflowers varies from blue to deep purple, but the garden cultivars have extended the colour range to include pale lavender and white. The Canterbury bell (*C. medium*) is a traditional cottage-garden plant which in the south-east of England has escaped into the wild and become naturalized on railway embankments and wasteland. It thrives on poor, dry soils and does well in front of the hedge. It is biennial and is usually sold as seed, which, if sown in late summer or autumn, will flower the following year.

If the area in front of the hedge is dry and in deep shade, the answer might be to plant one of the wood spurges, such as *Euphorbia amygdaloides* var. *robbiae*, a ground-covering perennial, about 45 cm (18 in) high, perfectly adapted to these conditions. It has dark green leaves and lighter, lime-green flower spikes in spring; it is also evergreen so will give all-year-round cover. Another group of plants that enjoy shade are the comfreys. The common comfrey (*Symphytum officinale*), with its pink flowers, prefers a moist soil as does the white comfrey (*S. orientale*) but both are good plants if you have room to let them spread. For a poor, dry soil, the rough comfrey (*S. asperum*) would be better suited. Rough comfrey was once widely grown as cattle fodder, and in some areas, farmers still cultivate fields of the flowers, which are pink in bud, but turn blue as they open, giving a two-tone effect. The comfrey most often seen on roadsides and hedgerows is the naturalized Russian comfrey (*S.* x *uplandicum*), which is also pink in bud, turning blue later. Both Russian and rough comfrey are big, bold plants with coarse leaves, but they look at home in a wild garden as long as they can be allowed to spread. *S.* x *uplandicum* 'Variegatum' adds a splash of brightness with its cream and green leaves and, if space is a problem, there are several compact garden hybrids, namely 'Goldsmith', which has gold-splashed leaves, and 'Hidcote Blue', a soft blue which turns white eventually. Both have a height and spread of no more than 45 cm (18 in).

One woodland plant that also works well in association with hedges is astrantia, as long as the soil in front of the hedge is fertile. The great masterwort (*Astrantia major*) is a bold plant about 60 cm (2 ft) high with shaggy flower heads in a delicate rose-green shade. The flowers are surrounded by papery bracts, which give the plant a distinctive appearance – they are often used in dried-flower arrangements. There are many garden cultivars and sub-species that either have larger flowers or different colouring, but all are in the white-pink-green spectrum. *A. maxima* has deeper rose pink flowers. If you need a smaller plant, *A. minor* is more compact at 30 cm (1 ft) high. The species astrantias can be left to self-seed around but the cultivars need to be divided in early spring as they don't come true from seed. All astrantias like a soil that is rich in organic matter, and will not grow on a poor, dry or stony soil.

USING CLIMBERS IN THE HEDGE

Even if the hedge itself is native, it works well to grow more exotic climbers up and through the foliage. They will fill out a gappy hedge or make a plain green one more interesting. It is a good idea to plant the climbers only when the hedge is well established, otherwise they may choke the young hedging shrubs. The new climbers will also need a bit of tender loving care until they are established. Choose sturdy container-grown plants that already have a strong stem – one- or two-year-old plants are ideal, and the stems should still be flexible enough to train up and through the hedge. Water new plants before and after planting and cover with a mulch to preserve moisture. In tall, natural hedges, climbers can be left to scramble freely and only pruned if they threaten to get out of hand. In small hedges they can be trimmed with the rest of the hedge.

If you want to clothe the hedge in a hurry, one of the best climbers is the perennial golden hop (*Humulus lupulus* 'Aureus'). It is fast growing and can cover a hedge in a single season, but it is also herbaceous so it dies back to ground level in winter. It scrambles through the foliage, rather like a clematis but the leaves are bigger and bolder and in full sun will turn a really golden yellow. For a flowering climber, the perennial pea (*Lathyrus latifolius*) is worth growing, particularly where its forceful twining growth can be accommodated. It has stout stems, not at all like the slender annual sweet pea, and the unscented purple flowers are prolific right through the summer months. There are various garden cultivars in shades of red, pink and white, and all will tolerate some shade.

Another group of good, but neglected, climbers for hedges are the tropaeolums, the best known member of the family being the annual nasturtium. One or two perennial members can be grown, including the flame creeper (*T. speciosum*), a hardy creeper with bright scarlet-red flowers in late summer and blue berries in autumn. Like the hop, it is herbaceous, but it will easily reach 3 m (10 ft) in a season. The yellow-flowered canary creeper (*T. peregrinum*) is a fast-growing but short-lived perennial (usually grown as an annual), which could be grown through a plain, south-facing hedge.

The summer-flowering fragrant white jasmine (*Jasminum officinale*) is more usually grown around an arch or trellis, but it looks stunning through a green hedge where it will twine and seek out the sun. It is very hardy and can be placed on any aspect. It could be placed with the winter jasmine (*J. nudiflorum*), which will display its yellow flowers from late autumn onwards. Both plants can be cut back to within a few centimetres of the base if they outgrow their space although, of the two, the summer jasmine is more rampant.

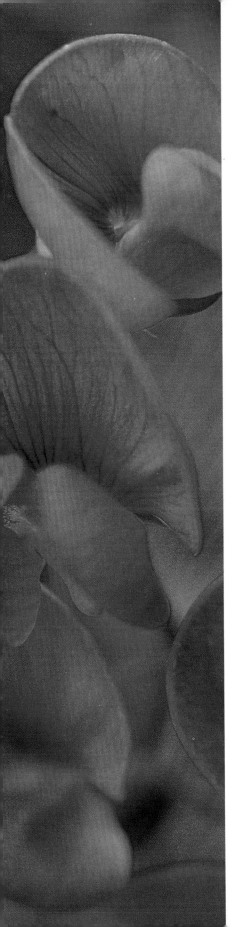

The wild honeysuckle is still one of the best hedge climbers, but if you want to ring the changes there are several more exotic species to try. *Lonicera periclymenum* 'Graham Thomas' is quite similar to the native species but with even more profuse honey-scented flowers. *L.* x *italica* has exceptionally fragrant early flowers, which are maroon in bud, opening to reveal pink and yellow petals. Also early is *L. caprifolium*, with creamy pink flowers that open in mid spring. For later flowers, try the Dutch honeysuckle, *L. periclymenum* 'Serotina', which starts flowering when the others have finished and goes on into early autumn. All honeysuckles enjoy a hedgerow habitat, because it allows their roots to be in shade and so stay cool, but allows the shoots to scramble towards the sun.

The perennial or everlasting pea (Lathyrus latifolius)

PAGE 152-3: Clematis *'Comtesse de Bouchaud'*

Most types of clematis, including the large-flowered garden hybrids, can be grown through a hedge and varieties like the early flowering creamy-white 'Henryi' look stunning against dark green foliage. For a more natural effect the choice is between the native *Clematis vitalba*, which has fairly inconspicuous greenish-white flowers and can be very rampant, and the later flowering Orientalis group, which are not quite as vigorous. The Orientalis clematis from China and the Himalayas produce small yellow scented flowers from August to October, followed by beautiful, silky silver seed heads. Also effective is the European *C. flammula*, which produces pure white, star-shaped, sweetly scented flowers in early autumn. It is best to avoid *C. montana* which, although it does an excellent covering job, will swamp the hedge, particularly when the hedging shrubs are small. Some of the herbaceous clematis are worth growing because the stems and foliage die back in winter and need no pruning. *C.* x *jouiniana* 'Praecox' is one of the best for scrambling through a hedge, with a mass of violet-edged white flowers in autumn.

HEDGEROW FLOWERS FOR DRY SOIL IN SHADE

HEIGHT X SPREAD

Betony (*Stachys officinalis*)   60 cm (2 ft) x 30 cm (1 ft)
Downy, toothed leaves; reddish-purple flowers, June to September; perennial

Hedge Cranesbill (*Geranium pyrenaicum*)   60 cm (2 ft) x 30 cm (1 ft)
Divided leaves; small mauve-pink flowers; June to August; perennial

Hedge Woundwort (*Stachys sylvatica*)   1m (3 ft) x 30 cm (1 ft)
Hairy, toothed leaves; reddish purple flowers, June to September; perennial

Herb-Robert (*Geranium robertianum*)   30 cm (12 in) x 23 cm (9 in)
Ferny leaves; small bright pink flowers, May to September; annual

Lesser Stitchwort (*Stellaria graminia*)   45 cm (18 in) x 23 cm (9 in)
Narrow leaves and stems; starry white flowers in clusters, May to August; creeping perennial

Self-Heal (*Prunella vulgaris*)   30 cm (1 ft) x 90 cm (3 ft)
Deeply-cut leaves; deep purple flowers, May to August; spreading perennial

Prunella grandiflora 'Pink Loveliness'   30 cm (1 ft) x 90 cm (3 ft)
Oval leaves; soft pink flowers, May to August; spreading perennial

Prunella grandiflora 'Loveliness'   30 cm (1 ft) x 90 cm (3 ft)
Oval leaves; pale, violet-blue flowers, May to August; spreading perennial

Sweet Woodruff (*Galium odoratum*)   15 cm (6 in) x 30 cm (12 in)
Umbrella-shaped leaves; starry white flowers, May/June; spreading perennial

HEDGEROW FLOWERS FOR NORMAL TO MOIST SOIL IN SHADE

Cuckoo Pint (*Arum maculatum*) 30 cm (1 ft) x 30 cm (1 ft)
Dark green leaves, spotted black; greenish-yellow spathe, marked with purple,
April/May; bright orange-red berries, autumn; tuberous perennial. Note: All parts of
the plant are poisonous.

Arum italicum 40 cm (16 in) x 20 cm (8 in)
Dark green leaves, white markings; greenish-white spathe, marked with purple,
April/May; tuberous perennial. Note: All parts of the plant are poisonous.

White Deadnettle (*Lamium album*) 40 cm (16 in) x 90 cm (3 ft)
Slightly aromatic nettle-like leaves; white flowers; April to September; spreading
perennial

Spotted Deadnettle (*Lamium maculatum* 'Beacon Silver')30 cm (1 ft) x 60 cm (2 ft)
Silver leaves; pink-purple flowers, May to August; spreading perennial

Lamium maculatum 'White Nancy' 30 cm (1 ft) x 60 cm (2 ft)
Silver leaves marked with white; white flowers, May to August; spreading perennial

Greater Stitchwort (*Stellaria holostea*) 45 cm (18 in) x 23 cm (9 in)
Linear leaves; square stems; starry white flowers in clusters, April to June; perennial

Wood Cranesbill (*Geranium sylvaticum*) 60 cm (24 in) x 35 cm (14 in)
Fresh green, deeply-divided leaves; violet blue flowers with white centre;
June/July; perennial

PLANTS FOR THE FRONT OF HEDGE BORDER (LIGHT SHADE)

NORMAL TO MOIST SOIL

Astrantia major   60 cm (24 in) x 45 cm (18 in)
Lobed, toothed leaves; star-shaped flowers, whitish green, tinged with pink, July; herbaceous perennial

Astrantia maxima   60 cm (24 in) x 45 cm (18 in)
Lobed, toothed leaves; pink flowers, July; herbaceous perennial

Astrantia minor   30 cm (12 in) x 30 cm (12 in)
Lobed, finely toothed leaves; white flowers, flushed with pink; July; herbaceous perennial

Common Comfrey (*Symphytum officinale*)   1.2 m (4 ft) x 1 m (3 ft)
Coarse, broad leaves; pinkish-purple bell-shaped flowers, May to July; rhizomatous perennial

White Comfrey (*Symphytum orientale*)   1 m (3 ft) x 60 cm (2 ft)
Dull green leaves; white bell-shaped flowers, April/May; perennial

Giant Bellflower (*Campanula latifolia*)   1 m (3 ft) x 60 cm (2 ft)
Glossy green leaves; lavender blue flower spikes, July; perennial

Sweet Cicely (*Myrrhis odorata*)   1 m (3 ft) x 60–90 cm (2–3 ft)
Ferny foliage; white flower-heads, May to July; black aromatic seeds; perennial

DRY SOIL

Canterbury Bell (*Campanula medium*)   75 cm (30 in) x 30 cm (12 in)
Basal leaf rosette; upright stems of blue or white bell-shaped flowers, May/June; biennial

Nettle-leafed Bellflower (*Campanula trachelium*)   75 cm (30 in) x 40 cm (16 in)
Nettle-like leaves; violet-blue flower spikes, July; herbaceous perennial

Euphorbia amygdaloides var. *robbiae*   60 cm (2 ft) x 60 cm (2 ft)
Dark green foliage; lime green flower spikes, March to May; evergreen spreading perennial. Note: Euphorbia sap can cause skin irritations.

Honesty (*Lunaria annua*)   1 m (3 ft) x 60 cm (2 ft)
Coarse, toothed leaves; purple or white flowers, May/June; silvery, translucent seed discs; biennial

Cow Parsley (*Anthriscus sylvestris*)   1.5 m (5 ft) x 60 cm (2 ft)
Fern-like foliage; flat creamy-white flower-heads, April to June; biennial or short-lived perennial

Pink Cow Parsley (*Pimpinella major 'Rosea'*)   90 cm (3 ft) x 45 cm (1.5 ft)
Fern-like leaves; flat pink flower-heads, May/June; perennial

Rough Comfrey (*Symphytum asperum*)   1.5 m (5 ft) x 45 cm (1.5 ft)
Rough, hairy leaves; flowers pink in bud, turning blue, May to July; perennial

Russian Comfrey (*Symphytum* x *uplandicum*)   1.5 m (5 ft) x 60 cm (2 ft)
Large, coarse leaves; flowers pink in bud, turning blue, June/July; perennial

HEDGEROW CLIMBERS

	MAXIMUM HEIGHT

Clematis 'Henryi' — 5 m (16 ft)
Mid-green leaves; large, white open flowers with brown stamens,
April to June; deciduous climber

Clematis flammula — 6 m (20 ft)
Mid-green leaves; tiny star-shaped white flowers, August to October;
deciduous climber

Clematis 'Bill Mackenzie' (Orientalis group) — 3.5 m (11.5 ft)
Mid-green leaves; open yellow lantern-type flowers, August to November;
fluffy seedheads; deciduous climber

Clematis x jouiniana 'Praecox' — 3 m (10 ft)
Coarse leaves; white flowers with violet margins, September to November;
herbaceous scrambler

Wild Honeysuckle (*Lonicera periclymenum*) — 3.5 m (11.5 ft)
Oval, mid-green leaves; sweetly scented cream flowers, June to September;
deciduous climber. Note: Berries are mildly toxic.

Lonicera periclymenum 'Graham Thomas' — 4 m (13 ft)
Oval, mid-green leaves; highly scented, creamy-white flowers; July/August;
deciduous climber. Note: Berries are mildly toxic.

Dutch (late) Honeysuckle (*L. p.* 'Serotina') — 4 m (13 ft)
Oval, mid-green leaves; scented, crimson and cream flowers, July to September;
orange berries; deciduous climber. Note: Berries are mildly toxic.

Early Honeysuckle (*Lonicera caprifolium*) — 4 m (13 ft)
Greyish-green leaves; scented pink and cream flowers, March/April; orange berries;
deciduous climber. Note: Berries are mildly toxic.

Lonicera x *italica* — 4 m (13 ft)
Oval leaves; very fragrant, maroon, cream and yellow flowers; April to July;
orange berries; deciduous climber. Note: Berries are midly toxic.

Golden Hop (*Humulus lupulus* 'Aureus') — 6 m (20 ft)
Golden leaves; pale green or yellow flowers, July/August;
herbaceous perennial climber

Perennial (Everlasting) Pea (*Lathyrus latifolius*) — 3 m (10 ft)
Narrow, dull green leaves; rich purple flowers, June to September; perennial
climber

White Jasmine (*Jasminum officinale*) — 8 m (26 ft)
Small, mid-green leaves; fragrant white flowers; July to September; deciduous,
twining climber

Winter Jasmine (*Jasminum nudiflorum*) — 4.5 m (15 ft)
Bright yellow flowers appear before the dark green leaves, November to February;
deciduous scrambler

Tropaeolum/Flame Creeper (*Tropaeolum speciosum*) — 4 m (13 ft)
Dark green, lobed leaves; bright red flowers, July/August; bright blue berries;
herbaceous perennial

Tropaeoloum/Canary Creeper (*Tropaeolum peregrinum*) — 3 m (10 ft)
Blue-green, lobed leaves; yellow flowers, July to September;
fast-growing annual

HEDGEROW WILDLIFE

Hedgerows are exceptionally good habitats for wildlife, providing both shelter and food. Twenty species of butterfly are thought to breed in hedges, including the wall brown and the brimstone – the bright yellow butterfly seen in gardens and along roadsides. Its caterpillar food plants are the buckthorn and the alder buckthorn, both of which are hedging plants. White admirals feed on wild blackberry fruit and flowers and their caterpillars eat the young leaves of wild honeysuckle, both of which are constituent climbers in many hedgerows. By including holly, dogwood and ivy in a hedge you may also attract the holly blue which lays its eggs on holly or dogwood leaves in spring and on ivy leaves later in the year. Interestingly, it is the ivy that is crucial to the holly blue and not the holly bush: if no holly is available, the adults will lay all their broods on ivy. Moths are dependent on hedgerows, particularly the pale yellow swallow-tailed moth, which lays its eggs on elder and ivy and can be seen flying around hedgerows on warm summer nights.

Many young hedgehogs are born in gardens each summer

A country hedgerow will house yellowhammers and warblers, but in the garden it is more likely to be home and larder to blackbirds, sparrows, thrushes, robins, finches and dunnocks. In fact, most garden birds will use a hedge as a convenient perch, as a place to look for caterpillars and other insects and as a nesting site. In the hedgebottom, wrens will delve about in the leaf-litter looking for insects. Thrushes, blackbirds and wrens like to nest from ground level up to about 2 m (6 ft) so a thick hedge is ideal. In urban areas where nesting sites are at a premium, the average garden hedge starts to resemble a block of flats with birds nesting a lot closer than they would normally choose to do.

Hedgehogs, of course, are the hedge's most famous residents. They may use the leaves at the bottom as a convenient place to sleep during the day, but at night they will travel across several gardens – and several miles – in search of food. They may also use the hedge to nest and give birth to their young, usually in June or July. During the winter, hedgebottoms are ideal hibernation sites and the hedgehog may stay there in a state of suspended animation for several months. For many small mammals, like the bank vole and shrew, the hedge is a vital corridor through which they travel to other areas in relative safety from predators. It is also a rich source of food, particularly berries, nuts, hips and haws, and innumerable snails and small insects.

As with many wildlife habitats it is the creatures we don't see that are the most vital to the ecology. Spiders, beetles and thousands of invertebrates go about their work unseen but are a vital part of the hedgerow system. The greater the number of different plant and shrub species in the hedge, the more diverse the dependent insects will be, and consequently the richer the hedge will be in bird and mammal life.

WHERE TO SEE...
HEDGEROWS AND HEDGEROW PLANTS

The best way to find hedgerows is to explore your own neighbourhood on foot or by bicycle if possible. The local wildlife trust in each county may be involved in the restoration of hedgerows and it is worth contacting them for details. The best hedgerows are not always out in the countryside and some good native hedges can be found in suburban areas, alongside roads and railway tracks. If you are concerned about a particular hedge or road verge, contact the county council to see what their plans are for protecting and caring for it. If people take an interest and show the authorities that hedges are important local features, they are less likely to disappear.

HEDGEROW HABITATS

Devon Hedge Group
c/o FWAG, Government Buildings, Alphington Road, Exeter EX2 8NQ, telephone 01392 428983.
A forum of organizations and individuals keen to promote the appreciation and conservation of Devon's hedges. The group organizes Devon Hedge Week and the Devon Hedge Fair, leads guided walks along Devon's hedgerows, and offers courses in hedge laying and the management of hedges for wildlife.

Kingcombe Meadows Reserve
Pound Cottage Visitors Centre, Lower Kingcombe, Toller Porcorum, Dorchester, Dorset DT2 0EQ.
Nature reserve with a wide range of habitats, including hedgerows.

Kingcombe Centre
Toller Porcorum, Dorchester, Dorset DT2 0EQ, telephone 01300 320684.
Educational study centre.

Berkshire County Council Roadside Verge Nature Reserves
c/o Paula Cox (Babtie Group Ltd), Shire Hall, Shinfield Park, Reading, Berkshire RG2 9XG, telephone 0118 9758844.
The public can contact the group for information about the scheme, or if they would like to recommend a Berkshire roadside verge for designation as a nature reserve.

Dorset Wildlife Trust
Brooklands Farm, Foreton, Dorchester DT2 7AA, telephone 01305 264620.
Local group, working to protect plants and wildlife in Dorset, including hedgerows.

HEDGEROW GARDEN

The garden of Daphne Cushnie (featured in the Hedgerow programme of the Channel 4 series *Wild about the Garden*) is open by appointment. For details, contact Clare Blight at The Devon Air Ambulance Trust, 01392 466666.

Chapter 6

Moun
Moor

tain
and Heath

THERE ARE TWO VERY DIFFERENT KINDS of heathland in Britain: the high moorlands of the mountainous uplands, found in the colder and wetter climes of Scotland and Wales, and the lowland heaths, mainly – although not exclusively – found in the warmer, drier parts of England. Within these areas there is an incredibly diverse range of habitats and micro-habitats that support very different plant communities. In understanding the minutiae of the way in which plants adapt to extremes of cold and heat, different base soils, periods of heavy rain or drought, we can learn a great deal about choosing the right plants for our own garden situations.

MOORLAND

To find moorland Britain we need only travel to areas where the land rises to over a thousand feet, as in Dartmoor, the Cumbrian mountains or central Scotland. The scenery is dramatically different from any lowland countryside we are likely to encounter. It is bleak and windswept, rocky, usually devoid of trees and characterized by a low-lying cover of vegetation on an acid, normally peat soil. It is one of the most primitive forms of landscape, relatively unchanged since the end of the last Ice Age. There is evidence that substantial colonies of pine, birch, hazel and even small oaks once existed on the upland moorlands,

Moorland has its own fragile ecosystem of plants and wildlife

that they were not always as treeless as they are now. Human activity, as always, has subtly changed the moorland landscape – although to a lesser extent than in most other habitats. Settlers have removed trees for their own use, attempted cultivation and latterly introduced the most significant factor for change: sheep. From 4500 BC to AD 1100 human activity here was a steady game of gain and retreat. Fields were cultivated higher up the fell or mountain when needed and left to return to moorland when they became redundant. It was only in the medieval period that the numbers of livestock reared increased and cattle and sheep became a regular feature of the moors. In certain areas, this was initiated by Cistercian monks, who in the thirteenth and fourteenth centuries took in thousands of acres of moorland for sheep rearing around the abbeys of Rievaulx and Fountains in Yorkshire and made large profits from wool. But on other moors, like Dartmoor, which had no great monastic houses, the economy of the moorland was more balanced. Here, cattle, sheep and deer grazing went hand in hand with peat digging, gorse and bracken cutting, iron ore mining and tin-smelting. It was in the eighteenth century that the landscape really changed to the one with which we are familiar today – a fairly empty vista of sheep and rough grass. In Scotland the introduction of new breeds of sheep, particularly the Cheviots, which could cope with the adverse conditions of moorland life, led to the bloody history of the Highland Clearances between the 1780s and 1850s. By the end of the nineteenth century, deer and grouse had been protected and encouraged by landholders as shooting game, and joined sheep as the predominant financial 'crop' of the moorlands.

Golden gorse (Ulex europaeus)*, also called 'furze'*

MOORLAND MANAGEMENT

The moors we encounter today are highly managed areas. The sheep keep the vegetation short, effectively clipping off any low-growing flowering plants and tree seedlings, but leaving clumps of tough tussock grass (*Molinia caerulea*) or mat grass (*Nardus stricta*) to grow long. Heather (*Calluna vulgaris*) is just one plant that will grow on unmanaged upland, but because it is a favourite of sheep, grouse and deer it is actively encouraged. To ensure a new crop of young heather, the moorland is burned every ten to fifteen years to clear away the mature, woody plants and encourage fresh new growth to come

through. Problems have occurred where either the moorland has been neglected and not
burned at all, or burned too intensely leading to the invasion of bracken (*Pteridium
aquilinum*) which shades out the heather. On upland moorlands the

*Clumps of grass cling to the
rocks of a fast-flowing mountain
stream in the Scottish highlands*

practice of encouraging farmers to have bigger and bigger grazing
flocks has meant that in some areas, especially the Welsh Hills,
heather is being overgrazed and is in danger of disappearing
altogether. The problem is being addressed by conservation
organizations, who have persuaded the Government to subsidize
farmers to manage their land differently, leaving areas sheep-free to encourage the
recolonization of moorland plants, including heather but also juniper, bilberry, saxifrages
and butterworts.

  Moorland is not a particularly endangered environment, but it faces many
problems of management and land use. We want to be able to walk in the Cumbrian
fells, the North Yorkshire moors and the Peak District but our presence causes problems
associated with erosion, litter and motor-vehicle access. New forms of recreation, like
mountain biking, are easing access to remote areas, but also increasing wear and tear on
paths. Moorland is under pressure from softwood forestry companies who argue that the
areas are 'wasteland' anyway. There is continuous discussion about the relative balance
between livestock, game and wild animals, like foxes and birds of prey. The actual
acreages may not be in mortal danger but we are no nearer to reaching a consensus
about how to sustain this fragile environment.

MOUNTAIN HABITATS

A mountain moorland contains many pockets of soils and vegetation, from peat bogs and
fast flowing streams (see Chapter 3) to short grassland or heath, cliff ledges and rocky
scree slopes. In the Scottish highlands areas of moorland have developed on a soft
limestone bedrock and illustrate how diverse moorland plants can be. The cliff ledges
here catch the fertile silt and soil that is washed down the mountainside by heavy rain.
Conservationists have identified two distinct planting environments: the wet flushes,
where the ledge is constantly drenched with water and the plants resemble those found in
bogs, and the dry flushes, where the larger ledges accumulate a good depth of lime-rich
soil, which has slipped from further up the mountain. These ledges are not constantly
drenched in water and soon build up a good layer of organic matter where leafy perennials
can colonize, almost like a garden herbaceous border. In other areas of the moor, where
the soil is thinner and the terrain more rocky, typical mountain plants, like golden
saxifrage, violet-flowered butterwort, yellow oxytropis, roseroot and mountain sorrel, can
be seen clinging to the rocks.

  In mountain areas, plants have to deal with great extremes – heavy downfalls of
rain, followed by periods of drought, extreme cold and blankets of snow in winter, wet
springs, short, dry summers and intense light through the growing season. Each plant is
intricately attuned to the environment and has different characteristics to meet the
demands put upon it. These mountain plants have to absorb nutrients wherever they

can, and often from water rivulets washing down minerals from higher up the mountain. The way plants propagate in this environment also reflects their opportunism: they set seed in the normal way, but the seed is washed tens, hundreds, occasionally thousands of feet down the mountain by the water. Likewise, plants like the golden saxifrage growing on the side of a stream can create new colonies when small pieces of the original plant break off and are washed downstream, to lodge in rock crevices where they can thrive on very little soil.

A fragment of heath in Dorset, a county which has lost 80% of its heathland in the past century

HEATHLAND

Lowland heath is a subtly different habitat from that of the upland moors. It is characterized by low rainfall and a shallow acidic soil which is light in colour, often fine and sandy in texture. Heath is colonized by low-growing shrubby plants, including heather, broom (*Cytisus scoparius*) and furze or gorse (*Ulex europaeus*). Heathlands occur in Dorset (Dorset Heath), in Norfolk and Cambridgeshire (the Brecklands), in Wiltshire (Salisbury Heath) and in the New Forest, Suffolk and Yorkshire. Occasionally the typical acid heathland soil gives way to pockets of chalk, where the light covering of soil tends to be alkaline rather than acid. This type of chalk heath is relatively rare but can be seen at Lullington Heath near Beachy Head and Newmarket Heath in Suffolk.

Heathland needs constant management if it is to survive. Most heathlands are man-made in the sense that they have been reclaimed from woodland and, over many centuries, have been cut, burned, and grazed by animals. Just like woodland, heathland was once a valued resource, protected as common land and used for grazing livestock and for supplying specific raw materials. Broom bark, for example, was used for tannin and to make rope, while gorse was cut and burned for fuel, and heather was used as 'poor man's thatch'. Bracken made good livestock bedding, and compost or mulch for the fields, thus helping to keep its naturally rampant tendencies under control. In the twelfth and thirteenth centuries, rabbits were introduced to heathland and large areas

were fenced to make 'warrens'. Rabbits were a hugely commercial crop and supplied great quantities of meat and skins, particularly in the Brecklands. If a heathland is not managed, the woodland species return, particularly oak, birch and beech which all survive well on heathland soils, encroaching from the edges gradually to eradicate the open space.

In many ways heaths are a much more fragile and endangered environment than the upland moors and mountains. This is mainly because they are nearer to the larger centres of population and there is greater pressure from housing and industrial development, roads and leisure access. It is easier also for conventional agriculture to take over lowland heath. With mechanized ploughing equipment and artificial fertilizers heathland soils can be upgraded to support cereal crops. Over the last fifty years Britain has lost 40 per cent of its heathland. The plight of counties like Dorset, where heath now

covers only a fifth of the area it did at the beginning of this century, is well known. Essex, whose situation is less well publicized, has lost its heathland almost entirely. It has become vitally important for gardeners to recognize that their own light soil and low rainfall could be a starting point for a heathland garden, and that they could play an important part in growing some of the plants that have lost their natural habitat.

Alpine viola (Viola dubyana)

Why should we worry about the disappearance of patches of scrubby heath? As with the many different habitats in Britain, it has a unique flora and fauna not replicated anywhere else. There are many different species of heather which are specific to some fragment of heath. The Cornish heath (*Erica vagans*), for example, is only found on the Lizard Heath in Cornwall and in Co. Fermanagh in Ireland, while the Dorset heath (*Erica ciliaris*) is local to Dorset, Devon, Cornwall and Co. Galway. Flowers like the heath dog violet (*Viola canina*) can only be found growing in a few scattered heathland locations, as can the pretty pale dog violet (*V. lactea*), which is confined to dry, acid heaths in the south of England and Ireland. Without heathland we would be denying a habitat to many butterflies, like the silver-studded blue and the heath fritillary, as well as to birds like stonechats and curlews that nest and feed in the low vegetation.

MAKING A WILD ROCK GARDEN

Many of us already garden on 'moorland' even if the garden itself is in a lowland area. If your garden has high rainfall and either acid or neutral soil, then in choosing moorland plants you will be gardening in sympathy with your natural environment and the garden will be less time-consuming and more rewarding. Many areas of western Britain, for example, have the high rainfall that suits these plants, and it is quite a simple matter to create a rock garden that will give them the drainage they require to live happily outdoors. More alpine plants are lost through waterlogged soil than through cold or frost. Winter hardiness can sometimes be a problem but is solved by choosing plants that grow in the colder, wetter parts of Europe and which will transfer successfully to British gardens.

A wild rock garden consists of large boulders and smaller rock materials known as scree. In the wild, a typical mountain slope might have a few rocks jutting out near the top, but lower down a layer of scree will have formed where the rocks have split, broken off and slid down the mountain. In the garden, a rock and scree area is a good disguise for builder's rubble, such as bricks, roofing tiles or broken concrete, which can be used as the base layer of the feature. If you don't have rubble available then you can buy stone from merchants, but do check where the rock has come from: there is serious concern that some, particularly limestone, is being taken from wild places in the north of England. The best source of garden stone is from a local quarry, where you can be sure that it has not been removed illegally and that it will complement the natural environment. It is senseless to import sandstone into a limestone area or vice versa: local stone will fit in with the surrounding landscape and make the garden features look more natural.

BUILDING THE ROCK GARDEN

Choose the site according to what is available in the garden. A natural bank or slope is ideal but rock plants will grow just as happily on flat ground, although the effect is not as natural. Remove any perennial weeds that would threaten to grow through the plants.

- ◆ Build up an artificial slope with rocks or rubble. This can be as steep or as gentle as the garden will allow. It is essential that a rock garden has this hard core of rocks or stones for drainage.

- ◆ On top of this under-layer place the large feature stones in position, jutting out from the slope; it looks best if the strata lines of the rocks are all running in the same direction.

- ◆ Make the top soil, with a mixture of garden soil or compost mixed with the same quantity of stone chippings or gravel: if the chippings are limestone this will make the growing medium more alkaline; if it is sandstone or granite it will be more acidic. This will, of course, affect the choice of plants. If you are unsure, it is worth buying a soil-testing kit and establishing the final pH balance of the soil: a reading of 7 or more will be suitable for the alkaline plants listed here; a reading of less than 7 is better for acid-loving plants.

PLANTING AND MAINTAINING THE ROCK GARDEN

It is best to use young plants, but allow enough room for them to spread to their final size. Use a trowel and firm the soil around the plants – water them in well. After planting, add a final layer of gravel or stone chippings: this helps to keep the drainage sharp, taking the water away quickly from the stems and leaves of the plants. Once planted up, a wild rock garden should need little or no maintenance. Plants that fail during the winter may not be hardy enough for your particular weather conditions and should be replaced with hardier types. It is worth finding out the native habitat of plants from other parts of Europe, Asia and New Zealand as this will give a clue to their preferred temperatures and humidity. Microclimates in gardens may defy the received wisdom that it is cold in the north and warm in the south, or dry in the east and wet in the west: it is worth assessing your own conditions and, rather than trying to change them, choosing plants that will be naturally at home.

A natural rock garden recreates the way plants grow in their mountain habitats
PAGE 171: *Campanula 'Joe Elliott'*

ROCK PLANTS FOR NEUTRAL TO ALKALINE SOIL

HEIGHT X SPREAD

Wall Daisy (*Erigeron karvinskianus*)   15 cm (6 in) x 40 cm (16 in)
*Grey-green lance-shaped leaves; daisy-like flowers turning white to pink,
May to September; perennial*

Mountain Avens (*Dryas octopetala*)   20 cm (8 in) x 60 cm (24 in)
*Glossy, dark green leaves; white flowers, May/June; feathery pink-silver seed
heads; perennial*

Alpine Lady's Mantle (*Alchemilla alpina*)   15 cm (6 in) x 45 cm (18 in)
*Divided green leaves, silver underneath; sprays of yellow flowers,
May to July; perennial*

Roseroot (*Rhodiola rosea*)   30 cm (12 in) x 30 cm(12 in)
*Fleshy leaved; pale yellow flower heads, May/June;
tuberous perennial*

Californian fuchsia (*Zauschneria californica*)   45 cm (18 in) x 45 cm (18 in)
*Long, narrow leaves; scarlet flowers, August/September; evergreen perennial;
not always winter hardy*

Pyrethrum (*Tanacetum densum*)   30 cm (12 in) x 30 cm (12 in)
*Silvery, grey-green foliage; yellow button-headed flowers, July/August;
evergreen perennial*

Campanula glomerata   45 cm (18 in) x 90 cm (3 ft)
*Dark green leaves; violet blue flowers, June to August; spreading rhizomatous
perennial*

ROCK PLANTS FOR NEUTRAL TO ACID SOIL

Gentiana septemfida   30 cm (12 in) x 40 cm (16 in)
Short, pointed leaves; deep blue bell-shaped flowers, July to October; perennial

Autumn Gentian (*Gentiana sino-ornata*)   10 cm (4 in) x 40 cm (16 in)
*Narrow, pointed leaves; blue trumpet-shaped flowers, September/October;
perennial*

Barrenwort (*Epimedium alpinum*)   25 cm (10 in) x 30 cm (12 in)
*Bronze foliage; dainty yellow and red flowers, April to July;
herbaceous perennial*

Mountain Pansy (*Viola lutea*)   15 cm (6 in) x 15 cm (6 in)
Oval leaves; yellow and violet bi-coloured flowers, April to June; perennial

Raoulia haastii   5 cm (2 in) x 30 cm (12 in)
*Tiny emerald-green leaves; carpeting plant with fluffy, buff-coloured flowers,
April/May; evergreen perennial*

Raoulia tenuicaulis   2.5 cm (1 in) x 90 cm (3 ft)
*Densely-packed bright green leaves; spreading plant with daisy-like flowers,
April/May; evergreen perennial*

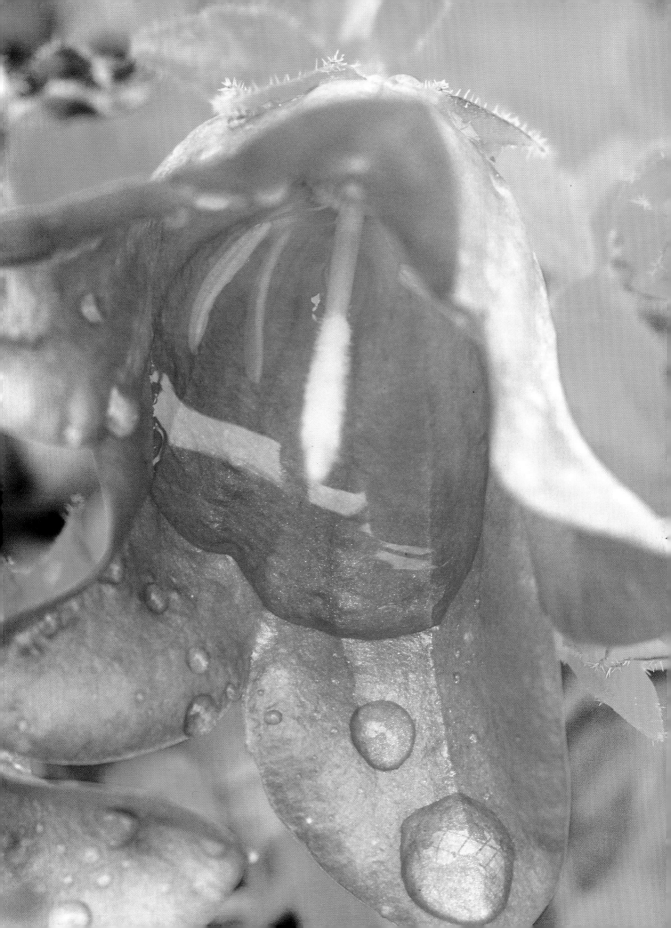

MOUNTAIN AND MOORLAND PLANTS

Mountain plants, or alpines, are probably the most misunderstood of all garden plants. At the end of the last Ice Age, Britain would have been covered in plants that can survive in Arctic conditions, but as the temperature warmed, these plants were restricted to the higher altitudes and to the more northerly parts of the country. True mountain plants find it difficult to adapt to growing conditions in lowland gardens, particularly in the south of Britain, which is why many 'alpine' gardeners actually grow European, South American or Asian alpines rather than British natives. All alpines share one characteristic: they cannot stand water around their roots. They need to be given very good drainage so that any heavy downpours to which they are subjected drain away quickly. Most alpine plants are low-growing, which helps them to resist buffeting by high winds and rain. They are ideal for exposed gardens and can be grown on high-rise balconies in tubs or containers.

ROSEROOT

Roseroot (*Rhodiola rosea*) is a native British mountain plant that is easy to grow in gardens. It forms upright stems of glaucous, fleshy leaves, topped by pale yellow flowers in early summer. It is very hardy and will form a clump of about 30 x 30 cm (12 x 12 in). Roseroot likes to be drenched with water but, like all alpines, it must be grown on a gritty soil so that the water will not rot the root. In the wild, it grows on mountain rocks, sea cliffs and screes on acid soil and chalk, and in the garden it will grow in quite poor soils. The rose-like fragrance comes from the root and can be detected when a piece is broken off. In its natural mountain environment, melting snow and landslides break the root into pieces and move them down the mountainside where they lodge in crevices and make new plants.

ALPINE LADY'S MANTLE

The alpine lady's mantle (*Alchemilla alpina*) is native to the mountainous parts of Britain and northern Europe, particularly on acid soils. It is a tiny version of the garden lady's mantle (*A. mollis*) with the same greenish-yellow flowers in summer, but more deeply divided leaves. It is a pretty plant, ideal for the smaller rock garden where it will grow to about 15 cm (6 in) high and spread to 45 cm (18 in) across.

ALPINE CATCHFLY

The alpine catchfly (*Lychnis alpina*) is now a very rare plant in Britain, due in part to over-collecting, and is now found locally only in the Lake District and Angus, in Scotland. However, it is widely available as a garden plant. It forms a tiny clump no more than 15 cm (6 in) across with a basal rosette of leaves and an upright flower-stem of rose-pink

flowers in the summer. Like most alpines it prefers a sunny position and a gritty soil. It is perennial and fairly short-lived, but it should seed itself around quite successfully. The closely related moss campion (*Silene acaulis*) forms a clump of moss-like leaves and has pink flowers in summer. Its natural habitat is on damp rocks where its cushion-forming habit helps it to remain stable in high winds and heavy rain.

Alpine gardens work best when they are in sympathy with the local landscape

ALPINE CINQUEFOIL

This Arctic-alpine species (*Potentilla crantzii*) is native to the mountains of Northern Europe but is becoming increasingly rare in Britain and is found only in local pockets of north England and Scotland and, very rarely, in North Wales. It is a true mountain plant, growing on the rock ledges and crevices up to 3000 m (9000 ft), and positively thrives on a rocky or gritty soil. The flowers are bright yellow with an orange spot near the base of the petals and they appear in summer on long arching stems. The foliage forms a mound about 20 cm (8 in) high by 40 cm (16 in) across – quite large for an alpine plant. The alpine cinquefoil prefers a poor, low-nutrient soil: in rich soils it will produce too much leafy foliage at the expense of the flowers.

ALPINE POPPY

Alpine poppies (*Papaver alpinum*) are small, dainty perennials with typical poppy flowers in orange, yellow or white. They are small (about 4 cm (1½ in) across) and the plants form a small clump of grey-green foliage. They are technically perennials and are usually short-lived but self-seed easily, particularly on gravel. They are excellent for bringing a touch of informality into a rock or scree garden.

STORKSBILLS

These members of the geranium family all like a dry, open situation and are small enough to be grown in rock gardens, troughs or between paving stones. The most widely grown species is the alpine geranium (*Erodium reichardii*), which has small white flowers with deep pink veins and will form a compact mound about 5 cm (2 in) high and 20 cm (8 in) across. Also good for rock gardens is the equally compact species *E. glandulosum*, which has purple-pink flowers and aromatic grey-green leaves. Storksbills take their name, like cranesbills, from the seed pod, which resembles a long, pointed beak.

ABOVE: Papaver alpinum

ABOVE RIGHT: *Erodium reichardii* 'White Sun'

GENTIANS

Mountain gentians fall into one of two groups: spring flowering and autumn flowering. Both have the characteristic vivid blue colour and grow in areas of high rainfall. In Britain, the wild gentian (*Gentiana verna*) is now exceedingly rare and a protected species, but it is widely cultivated in gardens. It is a mat-forming perennial that produces its rich blue flowers from April to June and is very attractive to bees and butterflies. It

copes with soils that are slightly acidic, neutral or alkaline as long as the drainage is good. There are two widely grown autumn gentians: *G. septemfida*, from the mountains of central Asia, and *G. sino-ornata*, from the wet mountain meadows of south-west China. The flowers of *G. septemfida* are long-lasting, beginning in summer and going on into the middle of autumn. The true autumn gentian (*G. sino-ornata*) can be distinguished by the stripes or bands of light green on the outside of the upright trumpets. Both autumn gentians prefer a slightly acidic soil.

ABOVE LEFT: *Gentiana* x *macaulayi 'Kingfisher'*

ABOVE LEFT: *Helianthemum 'Fire Dragon'*

SAXIFRAGES

There are so many mountain saxifrages that they almost command a book in their own right. The starry saxifrage (*Saxifraga stellaris*), with its white summer flowers, can be

grown in high rainfall areas. In the wild it clings to wet mountain ledges, or rocks by a stream, and needs constant flushing with water. Also found growing in the wetter mountain districts of Scotland, Wales and northern England is the yellow mountain saxifrage (*S. aizoides*) with its bright yellow or orange flowers, sometimes spotted with red. However, there are lots of garden species and cultivars that don't need continuous wet: *S. paniculata* is a good 'beginner's alpine', with silvery rosettes of foliage and sprays of white, buttercup-like flowers. It likes a limy soil but can tolerate long periods of drought. *S.* x *burnatti* likes the same conditions and is similar in appearance, although it has star-shaped flowers.

Bell heather (Erica cineria)
likes well-drained, acid soil

ALPINE AVENS

The alpine avens (*Geum montanum*) species is a native of the rocky mountain pastures of south and central Europe and will grow well in an open site, such as a rock garden, as long as it gets regular moisture. It forms a medium-sized clump of foliage and bright yellow flowers in late spring and early summer. It also has fluffy, reddish-brown seed-heads that extend the season of interest. The native mountain avens of Britain is *Dryas octopetala*, a similar plant but with white flowers and silvery seed-heads. Both species need well-drained soil and plenty of rainfall.

MOORLAND TREES AND SHRUBS

Several trees adapt well to 'moorland' garden conditions, including those that tolerate an acid soil (see p.19). Mountain ash or rowan (*Sorbus aucuparia*), with its bright red autumn berries, and the slender silver birch (*Betula pendula*) grow happily on well-drained soils and add structure to what might otherwise be a totally flat garden. If there is no room for trees, the native bilberry (*Vaccinium myrtillus*) of northern England is happy on dry, acid soils and makes a good garden shrub. In the wild it is found on moors and heath and in birch and pine woods, from Cumbria and Durham northwards, and the sweet blackberries of autumn can be made into pies and jams. It has a close relative, the cowberry (*V. vitis-idaea*), which is found widely on Scottish moors and has pretty small pale pink flowers and red, non-edible fruit. Both shrubs are compact, no higher than 60 cm (2 ft) and suitable for even small gardens. For rock gardens, the bearberry (*Arctostaphylos uva-ursi*) is a tough low-growing shrub with shiny red berries. It has small glossy evergreen leaves and the whole plant will eventually spread to 3 m (10 ft), so could be planted to trail over a wall or down a substantial rock bank. Bearberry is another northern native, found on the rocky moors and heaths of the Pennines and the Scottish Highlands and islands.

HEATHLAND PLANTS

In gardens, heathers have a bad name because they are often used in an over-formal way. However, they can work well in a wild garden, if you plant them in a way that is closer to their natural habitat. Heathers like an acid or neutral soil and their only real dislike is of a very limy growing medium. A naturally peaty soil is perfect for heathers, but if you don't have this, there is no point in digging in extra peat or iron supplements to make your garden more suitable. Accept the growing conditions you have and plant accordingly. Although heathers are mostly associated with cold, upland areas, they will grow in lower, warmer sites.

The common native heather (*Calluna vulgaris*) grows in a range of habitats, from lowland heaths to upland moors, the common denominator being the acidic soil. *Erica carnea* is one of the most widely grown garden heathers. It is a European alpine but grows well in British gardens, particularly at high altitudes. It is also more lime-tolerant than many other heathers, which probably accounts for its popularity. It flowers in late spring rather than late summer. There are hundreds of garden cultivars. Also popular is the bell heather (*E. cinerea*), which is native to Britain but which does need an acid soil. It is late-summer flowering and comes in a range of colours from white, through pink to deep purple. The Cornish heath (*E. vagans*) is very local to the south-west of Britain but is available as a garden plant although it must have a magnesium-rich soil.

Heathers can adapt to full sun or light shade, but will not grow in deep shade. They need to be planted closely together to give a dense carpeting effect, but they can also look natural set between rocks or paving. They should never be placed in straight rows and they rarely look good planted on their own.

HAREBELLS

The harebell (*Campanula rotundifolia*) is one of the prettiest late summer plants for dry banks or grassland. In the wild it will be found growing on roadsides, heaths, commons and downs wherever there is a light covering of usually sandy, but sometimes chalky soil. It is a common flower of Scottish uplands, but it can also be found growing in most counties except the south-west of Britain. If you have a light soil, this perennial can easily be naturalized in grass and makes an alternative to a full wildflower meadow. The fine wiry stems rarely look good in a border and it is more suited to rocky areas or grass. The plant grows from rhizomes, which should be planted in spring or autumn. Once established it should self-seed if the grass is left uncut until after flowering.

In rock and alpine gardens it is more common to see a close relative of the harebell, the fairy thimble (*C. cochleariifolia*), a low-growing, spreading plant with dainty lavender-blue bells. It is a native of the mountains of France and Germany, where it thrives on rocky grassland, limestone, and screes. It makes a pretty little garden plant, given good drainage and an open sunny position.

PASQUE-FLOWER

The pasque-flower (*Pulsatilla vulgaris*) is a typical plant of limestone downs and heaths, particularly where there has been grazing to keep the turf short, which allows the flowers to compete with the grasses. It blooms in late spring, creating a carpet of purple anemone-type flowers, but it has declined greatly in the wild due to the 'improvement' of heathland and the loss of land to development. It still occurs in pockets of East Anglia, the Chilterns and the Cotswolds. It blooms around Eastertide, hence its name; in Rutland it is called, charmingly, blue emony. Like all the heath plants, it likes sun and really good drainage but is happiest on a neutral to alkaline soil rather than acid.

BROOMS AND GREENWEEDS

This group of closely related plants includes the common broom (*Cytisus scoparius*) and its garden relatives, and the greenweeds (*Genista* species), with similar vivid yellow flowers. Brooms will thrive wherever the ground is dry, the soil neutral to acidic and the aspect sunny. The common broom makes a shrub about 1.5 m (4 ft) high eventually but there are many lower-growing garden hybrids which will stay at a similar height to heather, particularly *C.* x *beanii* (to 40 cm, 16 in) and *C.* 'Cottage', which has creamy yellow flowers and stays a compact 30 cm (12 in). The summer-flowering genistas are also suitable for sunny, dry sites where the soil is poor or stony. *Genista pilosa* has several garden forms, including 'Vancouver Gold' and 'Goldilocks', which are more compact than the species. Also, for dry areas the dyer's greenweed (*G. tinctoria*) forms a fairly large, informal shrub, although, again, more compact garden forms are available. Dyer's greenweed has long been used to extract green and yellow dye – in Gloucestershire, women pulled up the wild crop by hand and were paid by the hundredweight.

GORSE

Gorse (*Ulex* species) is a typical heathland plant, with its evergreen leaves and vivid flowers. It is known, quite rightly, as golden gorse, and although its main flowering time is late winter to early spring, it will flower intermittently throughout the year. It prefers a slightly acid soil but is found growing in a wide range of habitats from heaths to banks and roadsides – in fact, wherever the soil is poor and dry. The common gorse, or furze (*U. europaeus*), can be used as a hedging shrub as it grows quickly into a dense thicket up to 2 m (6 ft) high and has effective thorns. If there is no room for a plant this size, there is a more compact form, 'Flore Pleno', which is slower-growing. It reaches a maximum of 1 m (3 ft) high but is otherwise similar to the species. In the absence of trees in counties like Cornwall, gorse was harvested for fuel for baking and light industry, while the thorns were ground up into a meal for feeding livestock in winter.

HEATH VIOLETS

Where the soil is light, the gardener can introduce a range of pretty violets, which once established will self-seed quite freely. The first of these is the mountain pansy (*Viola lutea*), which grows naturally in short grass or on rocky ground and is found in the hillier parts of Britain. It is hardy in even the coldest winters. The flowers are yellow or sometimes violet or bi-coloured. The true heath violet (*V. canina*) is now a rare plant in the wild which grows on light, sandy soils and has bright blue flowers. Slightly paler blue is the pale dog violet (*V. lactea*), which can still be found on short grassy heaths in the south of England.

MOUNTAIN EVERLASTING

Mountain everlasting (*Antennaria dioica*), also known as cat's foot, is a native of dry, mountain grassland on limestone or neutral soils. It is widespread in upland Britain, and has a rosette of evergreen woolly leaves at ground level with an upright stem topped by a cluster of pink or white flower heads in early summer. It can survive at high altitudes, up to 3000 m (9000 ft), so should be suitable for the highest hill-top or tower-block garden. It likes a well-drained gritty soil and full sun. Several garden cultivars have been bred to improve the colour, such as 'Rubra', which has deep red flowers. The foliage forms a low silvery-white mat throughout the year, but the flower stems grow to about 60 cm (2 ft) high.

THYME

Members of the thyme family make good ground cover for dry, poor soils and have more to offer than their aroma and herb value. There are several wild thymes in the British isles, the most common being *Thymus praecox*, which can be found growing in dry, grassy places, on heaths, rocky banks, limestone pavements and even on sand dunes. In central and southern England the common species is the large or broad-leaved thyme

(*T. pulegiodes*), which is found mainly on chalky hills and banks. In East Anglia there is a very rare Breckland or creeping thyme (*T. serpyllum*), a low-growing plant, perfectly suited to the rabbit-grazed, sandy soils of Breckland. This species is the one that has been most widely adopted by gardeners, mainly for its dense, mat-forming habit, and many garden cultivars offer variations on the usual purple-mauve colour. All thymes, whether they are native or imported species, like a well-drained gritty soil and work well in rock gardens, between paving stones, or growing freely over stony ground.

Thyme and thrift grow well on light, heathland soils .

MOUNTAIN PLANTS

Alpine geranium (*Erodium reichardii*)   5 cm (2 in) x 20 cm (8 in)
Deep green, heart-shaped leaves; single white flowers with pink veins, June to August; perennial

Alpine Lady's Mantle (*Alchemilla alpina*)   15 cm (6 in) x 45 cm (18 in)
Divided green leaves, silver underneath; sprays of yellow flowers, May to July; perennial

Roseroot (*Rhodiola rosea*)   30 cm (12 in) x 30 cm (12 in)
Fleshy, succulent leaves; pale yellow flower-heads, May/June; fleshy leafed, tuberous perennial

Alpine Catchfly (*Lychnis alpina*)   15 cm (6 in) x 10 cm (4 in)
Rosette of dark green leaves; rose-purple flowers, May to July; short-lived perennial

Moss Campion (*Silene acaulis*)   5 cm (2 in) x 15 cm (6 in)
Cushion of bright green foliage; pink flowers, May; evergreen perennial

Alpine Cinquefoil (*Potentilla crantzii*)   20 cm (8 in) x 40 cm (16 in)
Dark green leaves; bright yellow flowers with orange centre, June/July; woody perennial

Alpine Poppy (*Papaver alpinum*)   20 cm (8 in) x 20 cm (8 in)
Grey-green finely divided leaves; white or yellow open flowers, May to July; short-lived perennial, usually grown as an annual

Spring Gentian (*Gentiana verna*)   8 cm (4 in) x 20 cm (8 in)
Short, grey-green leaves; vivid blue open flowers with a white centre, March/April; perennial

Gentiana septemfida   30 (12 in) x 40 cm (16 in)
Short, pointed leaves; deep blue bell-shaped flowers, July to October; perennial

Autumn Gentian (*Gentiana sino-ornata*)   10 cm (4 in) x 40 cm (16 in)
Narrow, pale green leaves; blue trumpet shaped flowers, September/October; perennial

Saxifraga paniculata   5–30 cm (2–12 in) x 20 cm (8 in)
Silvery green foliage rosettes; white flowers with yellow centres, May to June; evergreen perennial

Saxifrage x burnatti   20 cm (8 in) x 15 cm (6 in)
Silvery green foliage rosettes; upright red stems; white star-shaped flower clusters, May to June; evergreen perennial

Alpine Avens (*Geum montanum*)   15 cm (6 in) x 30 cm (12 in)
Deep green, basal leaves; bright yellow flowers, May/June; fluffy buff seed heads; rhizomatous perennial

Mountain Avens (*Dryas octopetala*)   20 cm (8 in) x 60 cm (24 in)
Glossy, dark green leaves; white flowers, May/June; feathery pink-silver seed heads; perennial

HEATHLAND PLANTS

Common heather or ling (*Calluna vulgaris*)   30–60 cm (1–2 ft) x 60 cm (2 ft)
Dark green foliage; purple flowers, August to October; evergreen shrub
NB: There are hundreds of garden cultivars that may be shorter or taller than
the species, and colours vary from white, pink, crimson and purple.

Alpine Heather (*Erica carnea*)   15 cm (6 in) x 40 cm (16 in)
Dark green leaves; rose pink flowers, May/June; evergreen ground-cover shrub

Bell Heather (*Erica cinerea*)   30 cm (12 in) x 50 cm (20 in)
Bottle-green leaves; bell-shaped pink or purple flowers, June to September;
evergreen shrub

Cornish Heath (*Erica vagans*)   60 cm (2 ft) x 90 cm (3 ft)
Narrow leaves; lilac, pink or white flowers, July to September; evergreen shrub

Harebell (*Campanula rotundifolia*)   30 cm (12 in) x 45 cm (18 in)
Narrow leaves; wiry stems; pale blue pendent bell-like flowers, July to
September; rhizomatous perennial

Fairy Thimble (*Campanula cochleariifolia*)   10 cm (4 in) x 60 cm (24 in)
Rounded basal leaves; pale blue nodding bell-shaped flowers, June/July;
mat-forming herbaceous perennial

Pasque-flower (*Pulsatilla vulgaris*)   20 cm (8 in) x 20 cm (8 in)
Pale green, finely cut leaves; purple flowers with yellow stamens, April;
herbaceous perennial

Common Broom (*Cytisus scoparius*)   2 m (6 ft) x 1.5 m (5 ft)
Tiny leaves; bright green branches; golden yellow pea-like flowers, May/June;
deciduous shrub

Cytisus x *beanii*   45 cm (18 in) x 60 cm (24 in)
Small hairy leaves; arching stems; deep yellow pea-like flowers, May/June;
deciduous shrub

Cytisus 'Cottage'   30 cm (12 in) x 40 cm (16 in)
Small leaves; upright stems; creamy-yellow flowers, May to June;
deciduous shrub

Genista pilosa 'Vancouver Gold'   45 cm (18 in) x 60 cm (24 in)
Small dark green leaves; golden yellow flowers, May to July; deciduous shrub

Dyer's Greenweed (*Genista tinctoria*)   1m (3 ft) x 1 m (3 ft)
Bright green leaves; golden yellow flowers, June to August; deciduous shrub

Gorse or furze (*Ulex europaeus*)   1–2 m (3–6 ft) x 1 m (3 ft)
Spiny shoots; bright yellow flowers, February to April and intermittently
throughout the year; deciduous shrub

Ulex europaeus 'Flore Pleno'   1 m (3 ft) x 60 cm (2 ft)
Spiny shoots; double yellow flowers, February to April and intermittently throughout the year; deciduous shrub

Heath Violet (*Viola canina*)   20 cm (8 in) x 15 cm (6 in)
  Heart-shaped leaves; bright blue flowers, April to June; perennial

Pale Dog Violet (*Viola lactea*)   20 cm (8 in) x 15 cm (6 in)
  Oval leaves; pale blue flowers, May to June; perennial

Mountain Everlasting (*Antennaria dioica*)   10 cm (4 in) x 60 cm (24 in)
  Woolly silvery leaves; pinkish-brown flower bracts, May/June; mat-forming evergreen perennial

Wild Thyme (*Thymus praecox*)   10 cm (4 in) x 30 cm (12 in)
  Oval leaves; purple flowers, May to September; creeping, mat-forming perennial

Common Thyme (*Thymus vulgaris*)   30 cm (12 in) x 30 cm (12 in)
  Dark green leaves; wiry stems; pink-purple flowers, June to September; shrubby evergreen perennial

Broad-leaved Thyme (*Thymus pulegioides*)   7.5 cm (3 in) x 20 cm (8 in)
  Dark green oblong leaves; purple-pink flowers, June to September; mat-forming evergreen perennial

Breckland or Creeping Thyme (*Thymus serpyllum*)   5 cm (2 in) x 30 cm (12 in)
  Dark green narrow leaves; mauve-purple flowers, June to September; carpeting evergreen perennial

MOUNTAIN AND MOORLAND WILDLIFE

Mountain and moorland habitats are home to some of the larger species of wildlife and although they are not likely garden visitors they are vitally important to the ecology of highland areas. Birds of prey are the most spectacular upland residents, such as the hen harrier, which breeds and hunts over northern moorlands, and the golden eagle, soaring over the mountains and moors in Scotland. Northern heaths and moorlands are also home to the short-eared owl, which is more commonly seen in daylight than other owl species, and to the merlin, the smallest falcon, which breeds in the west and north of Britain but is in decline.

The Scottish moorlands are home to unique colonies of wildlife

The typical moorland supports curlew, which roost and breed in the rough moorland vegetation and emerge to feed on the mud flats of rivers and marshes. It is a wading bird and can also be seen on the coasts, using its long curving beak to delve down into the sand. Higher up on the mountain top, and on shooting moors, there will be grouse and partridge. It is also possible to find ptarmigan, a small grouse-like bird that changes its plumage from pure white in winter to blend in with the snow to mottled brown in summer, which camouflages it against the mountainside vegetation.

Mountains and upland moors are also home to a surprising number of butterflies, including the large heath, which is found on hillsides and damp moorlands in the north

of Britain, and the small heath, in a range of habitats throughout the British Isles. Also common on upland moors is the marsh fritillary which, although it is typically found on wet marshes, also flies over drier, upland hill slopes, laying its eggs on plantain and devil's bit scabious.

Deer are the largest mammals to be found on the open mountainside and moorlands of Britain, most commonly the red deer or the smaller and lighter-coloured roe deer. Although they are technically wild animals, they are managed and controlled by shooting in most areas because of their appetite for vegetation – particularly young tree growth.

HEATHLAND WILDLIFE

Heathlands are surprisingly full of wildlife, particularly insects – there are thought to be over twenty thousand different insect species living on heathland in Britain. Most spectacular are the butterflies, like the silver-studded blue, which is found on heaths and chalk grassland in southern England and Wales. This delicate little butterfly is greyish-white or beige with its wings shut, but bright violet blue when they open. When the wings are closed it can still be identified by the spots at the margins of the wings, which have shiny blue-green centres that give the 'silver-studded' appearance. The caterpillars of the silver-studded blue feed on broom and gorse.

A much rarer butterfly of dry grasslands is the heath fritillary, now found in only one or two counties of southern England and a protected species. Like most fritillaries it has a rich brown, speckled colouring and feeds on plantain and grasses. Heathlands are also home to the small copper, which is widespread on open grassland and meadows, laying its eggs on dock leaves and sorrel. One casualty of the loss of heathlands and open meadows has been the large blue butterfly, declared extinct in Britain in the late 1970s but now the subject of an intensive species-recovering programme. Its favoured habitat is heaths and grasslands, particularly near the coast, where the adults lay eggs on creeping thyme (*Thymus serpyllum*). The young caterpillars feed on the thyme leaves during their first few weeks of life.

Heathland birds are more often heard than seen, although one to look out for is the stonechat, which sometimes perches on bushes or fences where it can be seen flicking its tail and wings. Rarer still is the tiny Dartford warbler, which nearly died out some years ago but has made a return to the gorse heaths in the extreme south of England. The lonesome cries of curlews can also be heard over heaths near the coast.

Dry heathland is perfect territory for snakes, and the smooth-skinned slow-worm, which basks in the warmth of the sun and dives into the light soil at the first sign of danger. Slow-worms also appear in gardens, where they are great slug-eaters and should keep pests under control. They need a place to burrow such as a hollow under a flat stone where they will spend their days, coming out after sunset to feed. Lizards also appear on heaths, though rarely in gardens. The common lizard is perfectly adapted to light, sandy soils which allow it to be camouflaged for most of the time. It feeds on flying insects, moths, beetles and caterpillars, and is found in many parts of the British Isles, particularly in the New Forest, although it is not common.

The rare sand lizard (Lacerta agilis agilis), found in only a handful of heathland locations

Rarer still is the sand lizard, only found in Dorset, Hampshire and Surrey and in the sand dunes of coastal Lancashire and Cheshire. Heaths may also be home to the only poisonous snake in Britain, the viper, or adder, which hides among the heather and heath vegetation feeding on small mammals and insects.

WHERE TO SEE...
MOORLAND AND ALPINE PLANTS

Many of the good upland habitats are in the care of the National Parks Authority, the National Trust (for England and Wales) or the National Trust for Scotland, who can supply details of the reserves and their locations. The Scottish Wildlife Trust is a voluntary organization that manages reserves throughout Scotland with a large number of local groups, working to protect plants and wildlife.

The National Trust Membership Department
PO Box 39, Bromley, Kent BR1 3XL, telephone 0181 3151111.

National Trust for Scotland
5 Charlotte Square, Edinburgh EH2 4DU, telephone 0131-226 5922.

Caenlochan Reserve, Clova, Kirriemuir, Angus, Scotland
Scottish Natural Heritage, 12 Hope Terrace, Edinburgh EH9 2AS telephone 0131-447 4784.

Exmoor National Park Authority
Exmoor House, Dulverton, North Devon TA22 9HL, telephone 01398 323665.

Scottish Wildlife Trust
25 Johnston Terrace, Edinburgh EH1 2NH, telephone 0131-312 7765.

ALPINE GARDENS AND NURSERIES

Bob and Rannveig Wallis
'Llwyn Ifan', Porthyrhyd, Carmarthen, Carmarthenshire SA32 8BP, telephone 01267 275205.
Nursery selling specialist bulbs and alpines.

Christie's Nursery
Downfield, Wetsmuir, Kirriemuir, Angus DD8 5LP, telephone 01575 572977.
Alpine nursery offering mail order with a good range of plants, including gentians and lewisias.

Alpine Garden Society
AGS Centre, Avon Bank, Pershore, Hereford and Worcester WR10 3JP, telephone 01386 554790.
For anyone in England and Wales interested in rock gardening or alpine plants. Entrance to shows, gardens, lectures, library, etc.

Scottish Rock Garden Club
PO Box 14063, Edinburgh EH10 4YE.
As above but for Scotland.

USEFUL ADDRESSES AND CONTACTS

Plantlife
The Natural History Museum, Cromwell Road, London, SW7 5BD, telephone 0171 938 9111.
Conservation charity solely devoted to saving wild plants and their habitats. A useful leaflet entitled Code of Conduct for the Conservation of Wild Plants is available from the above address.

English Nature
Northminster House, Peterborough, Cambridgeshire, PE1 1UA, telephone 01733 455000.
Statutory body, working in partnership with other organizations, including the Government, to promote and achieve nature conservation in England. Co-ordinators of the Veteran Trees Initiative.

The Wildlife Trusts
UK National Office, The Green, Witham Park, Waterside South, Lincoln, LN5 7JR, telephone 01522 544400.
Voluntary organization with a large number of local groups, working to protect plants and wildlife. Manages nature reserves throughout the country.

British Trust for Conservation Volunteers
36 St Mary's Street, Wallingford, Oxfordshire, OX10 OEU, telephone 01491 839766: web: http://www.btcv.org.uk/
Practical conservation charity providing volunteering opportunities to protect and improve the environment in the UK and around the world. They also run Natural Break, conservation working holidays: e-mail natural-breaks@btcv.org.uk.

FURTHER READING AND REFERENCE

Jackie Bennett, *The Wildlife Garden Month by Month*
(David & Charles, 1997)

Marjorie Blamey and Christopher Grey-Wilson, *The Illustrated Flora of Britain and Northern Europe*
(Hodder and Stoughton, 1989)

Geoffrey Grigson, *The Englishman'S Flora*
(Dent, 1955). Reprints and secondhand copies of early editions still available

Richard Mabey and Tony Evans, *The Flowering of Britain*
(Chatto & Windus, 1989)

Roger Phillips, *Trees in Britain, Europe and North America*
(Pan, 1978)

Roger Phillips and Martyn Rix, *Perennials*
(2 vols, Pan 1991)

Oliver Rackham, *The History of the Countryside*
(Dent, 1987)

The Readers' Digest New Encyclopedia of Garden Plants and Flowers
(1997)

The RHS Plantfinder 1997-1998
(Dorling Kindersley, 1997)

Oliver Rackham, *Trees and Woodland in the British Landscape*
(Revised edition 1990)

William Robinson, *The Wild Garden*
(1870). Reprints available

Violet Stevenson, *The Wild Garden*
(Frances Lincoln, 1985)

LIST OF PROTECTED SPECIES

The following wild plants and flowers are protected by law under the Wildlife and Countryside Act 1981. It is an offence to pick, uproot or disturb these plants in any way. The species include members of some of the best-known plant families – pinks, violas, salvias, gentians, saxifrages and orchids – all of which are now either rare or in danger of becoming so.

Plant	Distribution
Adder's Tongue Spearwort (*Ranunculus ophioglossifolius*)	Gloucestershire
Alison, Small (*Alyssum alyssoides*)	S. England, E. Scotland
Alpine Catchfly (*Lychnis alpina*)	Lake District, Angus
Alpine Fleabane (*Erigeron borealis*)	Scotland
Alpine Sow Thistle (*Cicerbita alpina*)	Scottish Highlands
Broomrape, Bedstraw (*Orobanche caryophyllacea*)	Kent
Broomrape, Ox-tongue (*Orobanche loricata*)	Bucks, Kent, Somerset
Broomrape, Thistle (*Orobanche reticulata*)	Yorkshire
Cambridge Milk-parsley (*Selinum carvifolia*)	Cambridgeshire
Centaury, Slender (*Centaurium tenuiflorum*)	Dorset, Isle of Wight
Cheddar Pink (*Dianthus gratianopolitanus*)	Cheddar Gorge
Cudweed, Red-tipped (*Filago lutescens*)	Surrey, E. Anglia, Yorkshire
Cudweed, Broad-leaved (*Filago pyramidata*)	S. E. England
Diapensia (*Diapensia lapponica*)	Invernesshire
Early Star of Bethlehem (*Gagea bohemica*)	Mid Wales
Fen Ragwort (*Senecio paludosus*)	Cambridgeshire
Fen Violet (*Viola persicifolia*)	E. Anglia, Ireland
Field Cow Wheat (*Melamphyrum arvense*)	S. England, Isle of Wight
Field Eryngo (*Eryngium campestre*)	Hampshire, Kent, Channel Is.
Field Wormwood (*Artemisia campestris*)	East Anglia
Fleabane, Small (*Pulicaria vulgaris*)	New Forest
Gentian, Alpine (*Gentiana nivalis*)	Scottish Highlands
Gentian, Spring (*Gentiana verna*)	Teesdale, Galway (Ireland)
Gentian, Early (*Gentianella anglica*)	Cornwall
Gentian, Dune (*Gentianella uliginosa*)	West Wales
Germander, Cut-leaved (*Teucrium botrys*)	Surrey, Hampshire, Glos.
Germander, Water (*Teucrium scordium*)	Devon, Cambridgeshire
Grass-poly (*Lythrum hyssopifolia*)	East Anglia, Channel Is.
Green Hound's Tongue (*Cynoglossum germanicum*)	Chilterns, Cotswolds
Ground Pine (*Ajuga chamaepitys*)	Kent, Hampshire, Surrey
Hare's Ear, Sickle-leaved (*Bupleurum falcatum*)	Essex
Hare's Ear, Small (*Bupleurum baldense*)	Sussex, Channel Is.
Jersey Cudweed (*Gnaphalium luteoalbum*)	East Anglia, Channel Is.
Lady's Slipper Orchid (*Cypripedium calceolus*)	Yorkshire
Least Lettuce (*Lactuca saligna*)	Essex, Kent, Sussex
Lundy Cabbage (*Coincya wrightii*)	Lundy Island
Marsh Mallow, Rough (*Althaea hirsuta*)	Somerset, Kent
Marshwort, Creeping (*Apium repens*)	Oxfordshire
Meadow Clary (*Salvia pratensis*)	S. England, S. Wales
Mountain Heath (*Phyllodoce caerulea*)	Scottish Highlands
Naiad, Slender (*Najas flexilis*)	Lake District, Scotland, Ireland
Naiad, Holly-leaved (*Najas marina*)	Norfolk Broads
Orchid, Early Spider (*Ophyrys sphegodes*)	S. and S.E. England
Orchid, Fen (*Liparis loeselii*)	East Anglia, S. Wales

Orchid, Ghost (*Epipogium aphyllum*)	Hereford, Shropshire, Oxfordshire
Orchid, Lapland Marsh (*Dactylorhiza lapponica*)	Scotland
Orchid, Late Spider (*Ophyrys fuciflora*)	Kent
Orchid, Lizard (*Himantoglossum hircinum*)	S. England
Orchid, Military (*Orchis militaris*)	Suffolk, Buckinghamshire
Orchid, Monkey (*Orchis simia*)	Oxfordshire, Kent
Pennycress, Perfoliate (*Thlaspi perfoliatum*)	Gloucestershire, Oxfordshire, Wiltshire
Pennyroyal (*Mentha pulegium*)	S. England, Ireland
Perennial Knawel (*Scleranthus perennis*)	East Anglia
Pigmy Weed (*Crassula aquatica*)	Invernesshire
Plymouth Pear (*Pyrus cordata*)	Devon
Purple Coltsfoot (*Homogyne alpina*)	Hebrides
Purple Spurge (*Euphorbia peplis*)	possibly extinct
Red Helleborine (*Cephalanthera rubra*)	Gloucestershire, Buckinghamshire, Hampshire
Restharrow, Small (*Ophioglossum lusitanicum*)	S.W. England, S. Wales
Rock Cinquefoil (*Potentilla rupestris*)	Wales, Scotland
Rock Cress, alpine (*Arabis alpina*)	Skye
Rock Cress, Bristol (*Arabis scabra*)	Avon, Channel Is.
Round-headed Leek (*Allium sphaerocephalon*)	Avon, Channel Is.
Sand Crocus (*Romulea columnae*)	S.W. England, Channel Is.
Sandwort, Norwegian (*Arenaria norvegica*)	Co. Clare, Ireland
Sandwort, Teesdale (*Minuartia stricta*)	Teesdale
Saxifrage, Drooping (*Saxifraga cernua*)	Scottish Highlands
Saxifrage, Tufted (*Saxifraga cespitosa*)	Scotland, N. Wales
Saxifrage, Yellow Marsh (*Saxifraga hirculus*)	N. England, Scotland, Ireland
Sea Knotgrass (*Polygonum maritimum*)	Channel Is., S. Ireland
Shore Dock (*Rumex rupestris*)	S. Wales, S. W. England
Snowdon Lily (*Lloydia serotina*)	Snowdonia
Solomon's Seal, whorled (*Polygonatum verticillatum*)	Northumberland, Scotland
Speedwell, fingered (*Veronica triphyllos*)	East Anglia
Speedwell, spiked (*Veronica spicata*)	Avon, Wales, Yorkshire, Cumbria
Spiked Rampion (*Phyteuma spicatum*)	Sussex
Starfruit (*Damasonium alisma*)	Surrey, Buckinghamshire
Stinking Goosefoot (*Chenopodium vulvaria*)	S., S.W. England, Channel Is.
Stinking Hawk's-beard (*Crepis foetida*)	Kent
Strapwort (*Corrigiola litoralis*)	Devon
Viper's Grass (*Scorzonera humilis*)	Dorset
Water Plantain, Floating (*Luronium natans*)	Wales, Shropshire, Cumbria, S. Scotland
Water Plantain, Ribbon-leaved (*Alisma gramineum*)	Worcestershire
Welsh Mudwort (*Limosella australis*)	Wales
Wild Cotoneaster (*Cotoneaster integerrimus*)	N. Wales
Wild Gladiolus (*Gladiolus illyricus*)	New Forest
Wood Calamint (*Calamintha sylvatica*)	Isle of Wight
Woundwort, Downy (*Stachys germanica*)	Oxfordshire
Woundwort, Limestone (*Stachys alpina*)	Gloucestershire, Denbighshire

This is not an exhaustive list and there are many more ferns, grasses, mosses and liverworts protected by law. Even those plants which are not listed here should not be dug up from the wild, and it is illegal to do so without permission from the landowner. More information on the latest additions to the Protected Species Schedule can be obtained from the wildlife trusts (see p. 188)

INDEX

Acer sp. 19, *24*, 131, 137
Achillea sp. 57, 60, 67
acid soil
    heathland 164, 167, 177,
      179
    moorland 160, 177
    peat bogs 75
    rock gardens 170
    woodland 19, 34
aconites 15, 38, 41
Acorus calamus 89, 92
agapanthus 118, 120
Agrostemma githago 65
Alchemilla alpina 170, 172
alder 19, *28*, 74
alder buckthorn 133, 137, 156
alkaline soil 164, 169, 170
Allium sp. *18*, 33, 40, 61
Alnus glutinosa 19
alpine avens 176, 181
alpine geranium 174, 181
alpines 167, 172–7, 187
Althaea hirsuta 76
amphibious bistort 88, 92
Andromeda polifolia 75
anemones, wood *15*, 33, 40,
    127
Antennaria dioica 179, 183
Anthemis sp. *56*, 65
Anthriscus sylvestris 21, 140,
    143, 148, 154
Aquilegia vulgaris 36, 41
Arctostaphylos uva-ursi 177
Armeria sp. 104, 107, *114*,
    115, 120
arrowhead 74, 77, 89, 91
Arum sp. 146, 152
Asplenium scolopendrium 23,
    27
Aster tripolium 101, 107
astilbes 77, 84, *85*, 92
astrantias *142*, *148*, 149, 154
Athyrium sp. 23, 25, 27
Atriplex halimus 110–11

barrenwort 23, 26, 170
beaches 102–3, 107, 115, 123
bearberry 177
bellflowers 34, *147*, 148, 154
Bellis perennis 62, 67
berries 19, 37, 128, 133, 134,
    137, 146, 177
Beta vulgaris 104, 107
betony 144, 152
Betula pendula 19, 177
bilberry 162, 177
birds *see* wildlife
bird's foot trefoil 48, 64, 67,
    68, 104, 107, 143
blackthorn 126, 130–1, 137,
    141
bladderwort 74
bluebells 14, *18*, 21, *31*, 33,
    40, 127
bog arum 89, 92
bog gardens 77, 82–7, 89,
    91–3
bog myrtle 75
bog primula 77, 85
bog rosemary 75
bogbean 77, *77*, 81, 89, 92, 96
borage 61
box 134, 137
bracken 162, 165
bramble *128*, 135, 156, 177
brassicas 100, 104, 107
Brecklands 164, 165, 180, 183
Briza media 57, 61
bronze fennel 61
broom 164, 165, 178, 182,
    185
buckthorn 76, 133, 137, 156
bugle 34
bulbs 37–40, 61, 66, 118, 187
bullace 131
burnet rose 111, 121

Butomus umbellatus 89
buttercups 62–3, 66
butterflies *see* insects
butterworts 75, 162
Buxus sempervirens 134, 137

Cakile maritima 103, 107
Californian fuchsia 170
Calla palustris 89, 92
Callitriche stagnalis 81
Calluna vulgaris 161, 177, 182
Caltha palustris 77, 81, 85
camassia 61
camellias *22*
campanulas *147*, 148, 149,
    154, *168*, 170, 178, 182
campion 34, 40, 100, 104,
    107, *119*, 147
canary creeper 150, 155
Canterbury bell 148–9, 154
Cardamine pratensis 66, 68, 96
carnivorous plants 75
catchfly 118, 172, 181
Centaurea sp. 57, 64, *64*, 65,
    65, 67
Ceratophyllum demersum 81
Cerinthe major 36
chamomile *56*, 65, 141
cherry plum 19
Chrysanthemum segetum 65
cinquefoils 75, 173, 181
clematis 15, 134–5, 143, 151,
    155
cliffs 103–4, 107, 110, 162
clover 48, *55*, 57, 64, 67, 104
Cochlearia danica 104, 107
Colchicum autumnale 16, 37,
    41
columbine 34, 36–7, 41
comfrey *148*, 149, 154
Convallaria majalis 26
coppicing 14, 28–9, 139
corncockles 50, 51, 65
cornfield flowers 50–1, 55–6,
    64–5
cornflowers 50, 51, *56*, 64, *65*
Cornus sanguinea 133, 137
Corylus sp. 19, 133, 137
cow parsley 21, 140, 143, 148,
    154
cowberry 177
cowslip 57, 62, 63, 67, 68
    giant 85, 93
crab apple 19, 37, 128, 137
Crambe sp. 102, 107, 116,
    119, 120
cranesbill 35, 41, 62, 67, 143,
    147, 152, 153
Crataegus monogyna 19, 126,
    128, 129, 130, 137
creeping Jenny 86, 93
Crithmum maritimum 100
crocosmias 118, 121
cuckoo flower 66
cuckoo pint 146, 152
curled pondweed 81
Cushnie, Daphne, garden 157
Cyclamen sp. 37, *37*, 41
Cytisus scoparius 164, 178,
    182

Dactylorhiza fuchsii 66, 67
daffodil, wild 49, 66
daisies 62–3, 67, 100
daisy busy 111, 121
Damasonium alisma 73
damp conditions 19, 40, 66
Danish scurvy-grass 104, 107
Darmera peltata 90
deadnettles 34, 144, *145*, 152
devils bit scabious 96, 185
Digitalis sp. (foxglove) 15, 34,
    35, 40, 41
Dipsacus fullonum 64
dog rose *130*, 134
dog's mercury 127
dogwood 133, 137, 139, 156
Drosera rotundiflora 75
dry conditions 19, 36, 100,

    104, 110–13, 114–16,
    152, 154
Dryas octopetala 170, 176, 181
Dryopteris filix-mas 34
dunes 102–3, 107, 110, 115,
    123

elder 19, 91, 126, 128, 133,
    137, 139, 141, 156
Eleagnus pungens 110, 121
epimediums 22–3, 26–7, 170
Eranthis hyemalis 38, 41
Eremurus x *isabellinus* 61
Erica sp. 167, *176*, 177, 182
Erigeron karvinskianus 170
Erodium sp. 174, *174*, 181
Eryngium sp. 102, 114–15,
    115, 120
erythroniums 33, 40
escallonias 111, 121
Eschscholzia californica 61,
    115, 118, 120
Eupatorium cannabinum 76, 77,
    86, 93, 96
Euphorbia sp. 60, 104, 107,
    149, 154
evening primrose 118, 120
evergreen hedging 134, 146

Fagus sylvatica 19
fairy thimble 178, 182
fenland 76–7
ferns 15, *21*, 23, 25, 34, 42
Festuca rubra 62
field maple 19, 126, 131, 137
Filipendula ulmaria 67, 86, 93
flag irises 77, 81, 88, 92
flame creeper 150, 155
foam flowers 23, 27
Foeniculum vulgare 61
foxgloves 15, 34, *35*, 40–1
foxtail barley *46*, 61
foxtail lily 61
Frangula alnus 133, 136
Frankenia laevis 103, 107
Fritillaria meleagris 51, 66
frogbit 74, 81, 88, 91
fungi 14, 21, 37, 42
furze 161, 164, 179, 182

Galanthus nivalis (snowdrop) 15,
    38, *39*, 41
Galium sp. 57, 64, *147*, 152
Genista sp. 178, 182
gentians 170, 175, 181
Geranium sp. 36, 41, 61, 67,
    147, *147*, 152, 153
Geum montanum 176, 181
glasswort 100, 101, *101*
Glaucium sp. 102, 107, 117,
    120
golden hop 150, 155
golden majoram 61
golden rod 61
gorse *161*, 164, 165, 179, 182,
    185
grass 47, 48, 52–3, 57, 62,
    161
Grass of Parnassus 86, 93
great burnet 63, 67
great masterwort 149
greater spearwort 76
greenweeds 178, 182
ground elder 146
ground ivy 146
guelder rose 19, 37, 91, *132*,
    137
gypsophila *109*

Halimione portulacoides 101,
    107
harebells 141, 178, 182
hart's tongue fern 23, 27
hawthorn 19, 126, 128, 129,
    130, 137, 141
hay rattle *see* yellow rattle
hazel 19, 133, 137, 139, 141
heather 161–2, 164, 167, *176*,
    177, 182

heathland 160, 162, 164–7
    plants 177–80, 182–3
    visiting 164, 167
Hedera helix 134
hedgerows 124–57
    climbers *129*, 134–5, 143,
      149–51, 155
    garden *129*, 138–9
    hedgebottom plants 143–6,
      152–3
    hedgefront plants 147–9,
      154
    plants *129*–37, 143–4
    roadside 140–3
    visiting 157
hellebores 25, 27
hemp agrimony 76, 77, 86, 93,
    96
herb-robert 36, 41, 147, 152
Himalayan balsam *87*
Hippophäe rhamnoides 110,
    121
Holcus lanatus 62
holly 129, 134, 137, 156
holm oak 106
honesty *147*, 148, 154
honeysuckle 15, 42, 134, 143,
    151, 155, 156
Honkenya peploides 103, 107
Hordeum sp. 47, 57, 61, 62
horned poppy 102, 107, 116,
    117, 120, 122
hornwort 74, 81
hostas *21*
Hottonia palustris 81
Humulus lupulus 150, 155
Hyacinthoides non-scripta 14,
    18, 21, *31*, 33, 40
hydrangeas *30*
Hydrocharis morsus-ranae
    (frogbit) 74, 81, 88, 91

Ilex aquifolium 134, 137
Impatiens glandulifera 87
insects *see* wildlife
Inula crithmoides 104, 107
Iris sp. 88, 92
ivy 134, 156

Jacob's ladder 67
Japanese maple *24*
Japanese painted fern 23, 25,
    27
jasmine 143, 150, 155
juniper 19, 162

kingcup 85
knapweed 57, 62, 64, *64*, 67,
    68, 141
Knautia arvensis 64

lady fern 23, 25, 27
lady's bedstraw 57, 64
lady's mantle, alpine 170, 172,
    181
lady's smock 66, 68, 96
Lake District 72, 160, 173
Lamium sp. 34, 41, 144, *145*,
    152, 153
Lathyrus latifolius 142, 143,
    150, *151*, 155
lavateras 113, 121
lavender (*Lavandula*) *109*, *112*,
    113, 121, 122
lawns 46–7, 52–6
leaf mould *18*, 21, 26, 42
Lenten rose 25, 27
Leucanthemum vulgare 55, 57,
    62, 63, 67
lichens 14, 21, 72
Ligustrum vulgare 134
lily-of-the-valley 22, 26
Limonium vulgare 101, 107
ling 182
Liparis loeselii 76
logs 21, 42
Lonicera sp. 134, 151, 155
loosestrife 76, *77*, 86, *87*, 93,
    96, *96*

Lotus corniculatus 48, 64, 67, 68, 104, 107
love-in-a-mist 61
Lunaria annua 147, 148, 154
lungwort 23, 25, 27, *85*
lupin 53, *53*
Lychnis sp. 66, 77, 86, 93, 96, 118, *119*, 120, 172, 181
Lysichiton americanus 89, 93
Lysimachia sp. 86, 93
Lythrum salicaria 76, *77*, 86, *87*, 93, 96

male fern 34
Malus sylvestris 19, 37, 128, 137
Malva moschata 57
marigolds
    corn 51, 55, 56, 64, 65
    marsh 77, 81, 85
marram grass 102
marsh mallow *76*
marshes
    freshwater 51–2, 75–7
    plants 84–7, 92–3
    salt 76, 100–1, 107
meadow barley 57, 62
meadow saffron *16*, 37, 41
meadow-rue 48
meadows 44–69
    annuals 55–6, 60, 61, 63
    converting lawn to 52–4
    cornfield flowers 50–1, 55–6
    management 57
    perennials 58–61, 63–4, 67
    road verges 140–3
    sowing new 54–5, 58–9
    visiting 49, 69
meadowsweet 67, 86, 93
meads 49
Menyanthes trifoliata 77, *77*, 81, 89, 92, 96
meres 73
milk parsley 96
Mimulus sp. 84, *86*, 93
Molinia caerulea 161
monkey flower 77, 84, *86*, 93
montbretia 118, 121
moorland 160–2, 172–7, 187
moss 14, 72, 75
moss campion 173, 181
mountain 158–87
    habitats 162–4
    moorland 160–2
    plants 172–7, 181
    wildlife 184–5
mountain ash *see* rowan
mountain avens 170, 176, 181
mountain everlasting 179, 183
mountain pansy 170, 179
mulch 18, 26
musk mallow 57
Myrica gale 75
Myriophyllum sp. 77, 81
Myrrhis odorata 148, 154

Narcissus 66, 143
Nardus stricta 161
nasturtiums 150
nature reserves 43, 76, 97, 123, 157, 187
New Forest *13*, 164, 186
Nigella damascena 61
Norfolk Broads 72, 73–4
Nuphar lutea 87
nurseries 43, 69, 97, 187
Nymphaea sp. *80*, 87, 88
Nymphoides peltata 87, 91

Oenothera biennis 118, 120
old man's beard 135
Olearia x *haastii* 111, 121
Omphalodes cappadocica 25, 27
orchids 62, 66, 67, 72, 74, 75, 76, 189–90
organic gardening 20, 97
Origanum vulgare `Aureum' 61
ox-eye daisies *55*, 57, *62*, 63,

67, 141, 143
oxlip 32, 40, 43, 85
oxygenating plants 81

Papaver sp. 50, 61, 64, 65, 174, 181
Parnassia palustris 86, 93
pasque-flower 178, 182
pea, everlasting *142*, 143, 150, *151*, 155
peat bogs 74–5, 162
penstemon 61
periwinkles *130*, 143, 146
Peucedanum palustre 96
Pimpinella major 148, 154
Pinguicula sp. 75
Pinus sylvatica 19
Plantago sp. 57, 103, 107
plantains 57, 76, 96, 100, 103, 107, 185, 190
Polemonium caeruleum 67
pollarding 29
Polygonatum x *hybridum* 22, *22*, 26
Polygonum amphibium 88, 92
ponds 73, 78–81
    water plants 87–9, 91–2
    wildlife 94–6
poppies
    alpine 174, 181
    Californian 60, 61, *115*, 118, 120
    field 50, 55, 56, 64
    opium 61, 65
    oriental 65
    Shirley 64–5
Populus sp. 19, 106
Potamogeton crispus 81
Potentilla crantzii 173, 181
primroses 14, 32–3, 40, 68, 85
Primula sp. 32, 40, 57, 63, 67, 85, 93
privet 134
protected species 189–90
Prunella sp. 57, 146, 152
Prunus sp. 19, 130, 131, 137
Pteridium aquilinum 162
Pulmonaria sp. *23*, 25, 27, *85*
Pulsatilla vulgaris 178, 182
pyrethrum 170

quaking grass 57, 61
Quercus sp. 19, 106

ragged robin 66, 77, 86, 93, 96
ragweed 141
Ransoms garlic *18*, 33, 40
Ranunculus sp. 62, 66, 67, 81
Raoulia sp. 170
red fescue 62
reeds 74, 76, 95, 97
Rhamnus catharticus 76, 133, 137
Rhinanthus minor 48, 57, 63, 67
Rhodiola rosea 170, 172, 181
rock gardens 167–9, 170–7, 187
Romneya coulteri 60
Rosa sp. 113, 121, *129*, *130*, 134, 137
roseroot 170, 172, 181
rowan 19, 37, 137, 177
Rubus cockburnianus 128
Rumex acetosa 57, 67, 68
rushes 74, 89

Sagittaria sagittifolia (arrowhead) 74, 77, 89, 91
salad burnet 64, 67
Salicornia europaea 101, 107
Salix cineria 19
sallow 19
salt marsh 76, 100–1, 107
Sambucus sp. 19, 91, 133, 137
samphire 100, 101, 104, 107
sandy soil 106, 108
Sanguisorba sp. 63, 64, 67

saxifrages 63, 67, 162, *163*, 164, 175, 176
scabious 61, 64, 68, 96, 141, 185
sea asters 100, 101, 107
sea beet 104, 107
sea buckthorn 110, *110*, 121
sea campion 100, 104, 107
sea clover 104, 107
sea heath 102, 103, 107
sea holly 102, 114, 120, 122
sea kale 102, 107, 116, 120
sea lavender 100, 101, 107
sea pinks *see* sea thrift
sea purslane 101, 107
sea rocket 103, 107
sea sandwort 103, 107
sea thrift 100, 104, 107, *114*, 115, 120, 122
seablites 101, 107
seashore 98–123
    gardens 104, 108–9
    plants 110–21
    visiting 123
sedge 75, 76
sedums 115–16, 120
seed merchants 69
self-heal 57, 144, 146, 152
service tree 127
sessile oak 19
shady areas 14–15, 21, 32–7, 152–4
shelter belts 106–7
shingle 108–9
shrubs
    bog gardens 91–3
    dry gardens 110–13
    moorland 177
    seashore gardens 106–7, 121
    woodland 14, 15
Silene sp. 34, 40, 104, 107, 173, 181
silver birch 19, 177
skunk cabbage 89, 93
snowdrops 15, 38, *39*, 41
snowflakes 143
soil
    enrichment 14, 15, 18, 21
    reducing fertility 108
Solidago `Cloth of Gold' 61
Solomon's Seal 22, *22*, 26, 190
Sorbus sp. 19, 37, 127, 137, 177
sorrel 57, 67, 68
speedwells 67, 143, 190
spiked water milfoil 81
spurges 21, 104, 107, 149
Stachys sp. 144, 152
starfruit 73, 190
Stellaria sp. 147, 152, 153
stitchwort 147, 152, 153
Stipa calamagrostis 61
stonecrops 115–16, 120
storksbills 174
Stratiotes aloides 74, 91
Succisa pratensis 96
Sueda vera 101, 107
sundew 75
sweet briar 134, 137
sweet cicely 148, 154
sweet flag 89, 92
sweet woodruff 147, 148, 152
Symphytum sp. *148*, 149, 154

tamarisks 111, *111*, 121
Tanacetum densum 170
Taxus baccata 135, 137
teasel *64*
thistles 141
thrift 100, 104, 107, *114*, 115, 120, 122, *180*
thyme 122, 179–80, 183, 186
Tiarella wherryi 23, 27
Tilia cordata 127
Tisetum flavescens 62
tree mallow 113, 121
tree purslane 110–11, 121
trees

heathland 165
hedgerows 126, 127
moorland 177
seashore gardens 106–7
woodland *15*, 19, 43
Trifolium sp. 57, 64, 67, 104, 107
Trillium sp. 40, 143
tropaeolums 143, 150, 155
trout lily 33, 40

Ulex europaeus 161, 164, 179, 182–3

Vaccinium sp. 177
valerian, marsh 86, 93
Veronica chamaedrys 67
vetch 143
Viburnum sp. 19, 37, 91, *132*, 137
Vinca sp. *130*, 146
Viola 143
    V. canina 167, 179, 183
    V. dubyana 166
    V. lactea 167, 179, 183
    V. lutea 170, 179
    V. odorata 38, 41
    V. persicifolia 76, 189
    V. reichenbachiana 38, 41
violets 14, 38, 40, 42
    dog 167, 179, 183
    dog's-tooth 33, 40
    heath 167, 170, 179, 183
    water 76, 81
Virginia creeper 143

wall daisy 170
water crowfoot 81
water dropwort 76
water forget-me-not 76
water lilies 74, 76, 77, *80*, 87, 88, *89*, 91
water meadows 51–2, 75
water plants 81, 87–9, 91–2
water soldiers 74, 91
water starwort 81
wayfaring tree 137
wetland 70–97
wild cabbage 104, 107
wild cherry 137
wild garlic *18*, 33, 40
wild plum 131
wild strawberries 143
wildlife
    heathland 167, 185, 185–6, 186
    hedgerows 126, 133, 134, 141, 156
    meadows 48, 52, 60, 64, 68
    moorland 184–5
    mountain 184, 184–5
    organizations 43, 97, 157, 187, 188
    seashore 100, 122
    wetlands 72, 73, 74, 76, 86, 94–6, 95–6, 96
    woodland 21, 26, 34, 42
wildwood 13–14
willow 74, 76
willowherb 140, 143
windy areas 100, 104, 106–7, 172
wood lily 40
woodland 10–43
    ecology 13–15
    garden 14–15, 20–7
    glades and paths 30
    perennials 26–7, 40–1
    planting 17–19, 26–7
    plants 32–7, 38, 40–1
    trees *15*, 19, 43
woundwort 144, 152, 190

yarrow *55*, 57, 67, 68
yellow archangel 34, 41
yellow oat grass 62
yellow rattle 48, 57, 63, 67
yew *135*, 137
Yorkshire fog 62

Zauschneria californica 170